PERSONALITY
Plus

What makes *you* so special?

A lot of things. Find out just how wonderfully and creatively God made you in *Personality Plus*. In these pages you'll learn whether you're:

- a spontaneous, vivacious, cheerful Sanguine
- a thoughtful, faithful, persistent Melancholy
- an adventurous, persuasive, confident Choleric
- a friendly, patient, contented Phlegmatic

or a combination of the above. You'll also learn how to best use these unique, God-given assets to bring harmony into all your relationships. Florence Littauer explains, "When we know who we are and why we act the way we do, we can begin to understand our inner selves, improve our personalities, and learn to get along with others."

Once you understand how to bring out *your* best, you'll find that others look better too. Discover the person you've always wanted to be in *Personality Plus*.

REVISED AND EXPANDED EDITION

PERSONALITY *Plus*

FLORENCE LITTAUER

Fleming H. Revell
A Division of Baker Book House Co
Grand Rapids, Michigan 49516

Library of Congress Cataloging-in-Publication Data

Littauer, Florence.
    Personality plus / Florence Littauer.
        p.   cm.
    ISBN 0-8007-5445-X
    1. Personality. 2. Temperament. 3. Success—Religious aspects—Christianity. 4. Christian life—1960- I. Title.
    BF698.L54 1992
    155.2'6—dc20   92-13275

Unless otherwise identified, Bible quotations in this volume are from the King James Version of the Bible.

Bible quotations identified GNB are from the Good News Bible—Old Testament: Copyright © American Bible Society, 1976; New Testament: Copyright © American Bible Society, 1966, 1971, 1976.

Scripture quotations identified TLB are taken from *The Living Bible,* Copyright © 1971 by Tyndale House Publishers, Inc., Wheaton, IL 60189. All rights reserved. Used by permission.

The Personality Profile is from *After Every Wedding Comes a Marriage* by Florence Littauer. Copyright © 1981, Harvest House Publishers, 1075 Arrowsmith, Eugene, OR 97402.

For current information about all releases from Baker Book House, visit our web site:
http://www.bakerbooks.com/

Contents

6   CONTENTS

A Special Note of Thanks

Twenty-five years ago a friend of mine gave me a copy of *Spirit Controlled Temperament* by Tim LaHaye and asked me to read it. I was instantly fascinated with the four temperaments that originated with Hippocrates four hundred years before Christ was born. As I read on, I found the description of a person so like me, and then one so like Fred, that I felt the author must have secretly known us. Although I had never met Tim LaHaye, I really wanted to talk with a man of his perception. Within a year our paths crossed, and we both spoke at the same seminar. Tim was just as dynamic and exciting as I'd hoped he'd be, and he encouraged me in my further study of the temperaments.

After all these years of teaching and counseling, I have put together my compilation of *Personality Plus* temperaments, and I am dedicating this book to *Tim LaHaye*, who first inspired me. I agree with what he said to me in a letter:

> I am more convinced now than when I wrote the book that the four-temperament theory is the best explanation of human behavior there is.

Thank you, Tim LaHaye, for your encouragement.

FLORENCE LITTAUER

PART ONE

Personality Profile

A Quick Method of Self-Examination

CHAPTER **1**

There's Only One You

Everyone wants a better personality. We all picture ourselves on Fantasy Island, where the ringing of the mission bells transforms us into articulate, attractively attired aristocrats. We no longer trip, fumble, spill, or grope; we converse, captivate, charm, and inspire. When the show is over, we switch off our mind-set and resume our test pattern of life. As we stare at our blank screens, we wonder why our "situation comedy" was canceled; why we've been replaced by the new stars who play their roles with confidence; why we seem to be cast as misfits.

We rush off to personality courses that promise to transform us into sparkling wits within twenty-four hours; self-evaluation experiences that will make us into minigods with maxipower; or sensitivity sessions, where we will feel our way into a fantastic future. We go expecting miracles and come home disappointed. We don't fit the mold of the exciting person, bursting with potential, pictured as the norm. We have different drives, abilities, and personalities—and we can't be treated as the same.

No Two Alike

If we were all identical eggs in a carton, a giant mother hen could warm us up and turn us into slick chicks or roving roosters overnight; but we are all different. We were all born with our own set of strengths and weaknesses, and no magic formula works wonders for all of us. Until we recognize our uniqueness, we can't understand how people can sit in the same seminar with the same speaker for the same amount of time and all achieve different degrees of success.

Personality Plus looks at each one of us as an individual blend of the four basic temperaments and encourages us to get acquainted with the *real me* underneath before trying to change what shows on the surface.

It's What's Underneath That Counts

When Michelangelo was ready to carve the statue of David, he spent a long time in selecting the marble, for he knew the quality of the raw material would determine the beauty of the finished product. He knew he could change the shape of the stone, but he couldn't transform the basic ingredient.

Every masterpiece he made was unique, for even if he had wanted to, he would not have been able to find a duplicate piece of marble. Even if he cut a block from the same quarry, it wouldn't have been exactly the same. Similar, yes, but not the same.

Each One of Us Is Unique

We started out with a combination of ingredients that made us different from our brothers and our sisters. Over the years people have chiseled on us, chipped, hammered, sanded, and buffed. Just when we thought we were finished products, someone would start shaping us up again. Occasionally we'd enjoy a day in the park, when everyone who passed by admired us and stroked us, but at other times we were ridiculed, analyzed, or ignored.

We were all born with our own temperament traits, our raw material, our own kind of rock. Some of us are granite, some marble, some alabaster, some sandstone. Our type of rock doesn't change, but our shapes can be altered. So it is with our personalities. We start with our own set of inborn traits. Some of our qualities are beautiful with strains of gold. Some are blemished with fault lines of gray. Our circumstances, IQ, nationality, economics, environment, and parental influence can mold our personalities, but the rock underneath remains the same.

My temperament is the real *me*; my personality is the dress I put on over me. I can look in the mirror in the morning and see a plain face, straight hair, and a bulgy body. That's the real me. Gratefully, within an hour I can apply makeup to create a colorful face; I can plug in the curling iron to fluff up my hair; and I can put on a flattering dress to camouflage too many curves. I've taken the real me and dressed it up, but I haven't permanently changed what's underneath.

If only we could understand ourselves:

Know *what* we're made of
Know *who* we really are
Know *why* we react as we do
Know our *strengths* and how to amplify them
Know our *weaknesses* and how to overcome them

We can! *Personality Plus* will show us how to examine ourselves, how to polish up our strengths, and how to chip away our weaknesses. When we know who we are and why we act the way we do, we can begin to understand our inner selves, improve our personalities, and learn to get along with others. We are not going to try to imitate someone else, put on a brighter dress or new tie, or cry over the kind of stone we're made from. We're going to do the very best we can with the raw material available.

In recent years manufacturers have found ways to duplicate some of the classic statues, and in any large gift store you may find dozens of Davids, walls of Washingtons, lines of Lincolns, replicas of Reagan, and clones of Cleopatra. Imitations abound, but there's only one *you*.

Where Do We Start?

How many of you have a Michelangelo complex? How many of you look at other people as raw material, ready to be carved up by your expert hand? How many of you can think of at least one person whom you could really shape up if only he'd listen to your words of wisdom? How anxious is he to hear from you?

If it were possible to remake other people, my husband, Fred, and I would be perfect, for we set out to chip away at each other right from the beginning. I knew that if he'd loosen up and have fun, we could have a good marriage; but *he* wanted me to straighten up and get organized. On our honeymoon I found out Fred and I didn't even agree on eating grapes!

I always enjoyed plunking a whole bunch of cold, green grapes beside me and plucking off whichever one appealed to me. Until I married Fred, I didn't know there were "Grape Rules." I didn't know each simple pleasure in life had a so-called right way. Fred first brought up the Grape Rule as I was sitting on the patio outside our cottage at Cambridge Beaches in Bermuda, looking out to sea and absentmindedly pulling grapes off a large bunch. I didn't realize Fred was analyzing my unsystematic eating of the fruit until he asked, "Do you like grapes?"

"Oh, I love grapes!"

"Then I assume you'd like to know how to eat them correctly?"

On that I snapped out of my romantic reveries and asked a question that subsequently became a part of a regular routine: "What did I do wrong?"

"It's not that you're doing it *wrong*; you're just *not* doing it right." I couldn't see that there was much of a difference, but I phrased it his way.

"What am I not doing right?"

"Anyone knows that to eat grapes properly, you cut off a little bunch at a time, like this."

Fred pulled out his nail clippers and snipped off a small cluster of grapes, which he set before me.

As he stood smugly staring down at me, I asked, "Does this make them taste better?"

"It's not for taste. It's so the large bunch will keep its looks longer. The way *you* eat them—just grabbing grapes here and there—leaves the bunch a wreck. Look at what you've done to it! See all those tiny bare stems, sticking up all over the place? They ruin the shape of the whole bunch." I glanced around the secluded patio to see if there was some hidden group of grape judges waiting to enter my bunch in a contest, but seeing none, I said, "Who cares?"

I had not yet learned that "Who cares?" was not a statement to make to Fred, because it caused him to turn red and sigh with hopelessness, "*I* care, and that should be enough."

Fred did really care about every detail in life, and my presence in his family did seem to ruin the shape of the whole bunch. To help me out, Fred diligently set out to improve me. Instead of appreciating his wisdom, I tried to sabotage his strategy and subtly change him to become more like me. For years Fred chiseled and chipped away at my failures—and I sanded steadily on his fault lines—but neither one of us improved.

It was not until we first read *Spirit Controlled Temperament* (Tyndale House) by Tim LaHaye that our eyes were opened to what we were doing. Each of us was trying to remake the other. We didn't realize someone could be different and still not be wrong. I found I am a Popular Sanguine who loves fun and excitement; Fred is a Perfect Melancholy who wants life to be serious and orderly.

As we began to read and study the temperaments further, we discovered we were both also somewhat Powerful Choleric, the type who is always right and knows *everything*. No wonder we didn't get along! Not only were we opposites in our personalities and interests in life, but each one of us knew we were the only one who was right. Can you picture such a marriage?

What a relief it was to find there *was* hope for us; we *could* understand each other's temperaments and accept each other's personalities. As our lives changed, we began to teach, research, and write on the temperaments. *Personality Plus* is the culmination of twenty-five years of seminar speaking, personality counseling, and day-by-day observation of people's temperaments. This book will provide a quick psychology lesson in easy, enjoyable terms so that we may:

1. Examine our own strengths and weaknesses and learn how to accentuate our positives and eliminate our negatives.
2. Understand other people and realize that just because others are different does not make them wrong.

To find our own raw material and understand our basic natures, we will examine the personality or temperament groupings first established by Hippocrates twenty-four hundred years ago. We will have fun with the Popular Sanguines, who exude enthusiasm. We'll get serious with the Perfect Melancholies, who strive for perfection in all things. We'll charge forth with the Powerful Cholerics, who are born leaders. And we'll relax with the Peaceful Phlegmatics, who are happily reconciled to life. No matter who we are, we have something to learn from each of these types.

Your Personality Profile

Directions—*In each* of the following rows of *four words across*, place an X in front of the *one* word that most often applies to you. Continue through all forty lines; be sure each number is marked. If you are not sure which word "most applies," ask a spouse or a friend, and think of what your answer would have been *when you were a child*. (Full definitions for each of these words begin on page 195.)

Strengths

1 ___ Adventurous	___ Adaptable	___ Animated	___ Analytical
2 ___ Persistent	___ Playful	___ Persuasive	___ Peaceful
3 ___ Submissive	___ Self-sacrificing	___ Sociable	___ Strong-willed
4 ___ Considerate	___ Controlled	___ Competitive	___ Convincing
5 ___ Refreshing	___ Respectful	___ Reserved	___ Resourceful
6 ___ Satisfied	___ Sensitive	___ Self-reliant	___ Spirited
7 ___ Planner	___ Patient	___ Positive	___ Promoter
8 ___ Sure	___ Spontaneous	___ Scheduled	___ Shy
9 ___ Orderly	___ Obliging	___ Outspoken	___ Optimistic
10 ___ Friendly	___ Faithful	___ Funny	___ Forceful
11 ___ Daring	___ Delightful	___ Diplomatic	___ Detailed
12 ___ Cheerful	___ Consistent	___ Cultured	___ Confident
13 ___ Idealistic	___ Independent	___ Inoffensive	___ Inspiring
14 ___ Demonstrative	___ Decisive	___ Dry humor	___ Deep
15 ___ Mediator	___ Musical	___ Mover	___ Mixes easily
16 ___ Thoughtful	___ Tenacious	___ Talker	___ Tolerant
17 ___ Listener	___ Loyal	___ Leader	___ Lively
18 ___ Contented	___ Chief	___ Chartmaker	___ Cute
19 ___ Perfectionist	___ Pleasant	___ Productive	___ Popular
20 ___ Bouncy	___ Bold	___ Behaved	___ Balanced

Weaknesses

21 ___ Blank	___ Bashful	___ Brassy	___ Bossy
22 ___ Undisciplined	___ Unsympathetic	___ Unenthusiastic	___ Unforgiving
23 ___ Reticent	___ Resentful	___ Resistant	___ Repetitious
24 ___ Fussy	___ Fearful	___ Forgetful	___ Frank
25 ___ Impatient	___ Insecure	___ Indecisive	___ Interrupts
26 ___ Unpopular	___ Uninvolved	___ Unpredictable	___ Unaffectionate
27 ___ Headstrong	___ Haphazard	___ Hard to please	___ Hesitant
28 ___ Plain	___ Pessimistic	___ Proud	___ Permissive
29 ___ Angered easily	___ Aimless	___ Argumentative	___ Alienated
30 ___ Naive	___ Negative attitude	___ Nervy	___ Nonchalant
31 ___ Worrier	___ Withdrawn	___ Workaholic	___ Wants credit
32 ___ Too sensitive	___ Tactless	___ Timid	___ Talkative
33 ___ Doubtful	___ Disorganized	___ Domineering	___ Depressed
34 ___ Inconsistent	___ Introvert	___ Intolerant	___ Indifferent
35 ___ Messy	___ Moody	___ Mumbles	___ Manipulative
36 ___ Slow	___ Stubborn	___ Show-off	___ Skeptical
37 ___ Loner	___ Lord over others	___ Lazy	___ Loud
38 ___ Sluggish	___ Suspicious	___ Short-tempered	___ Scatterbrained
39 ___ Revengeful	___ Restless	___ Reluctant	___ Rash
40 ___ Compromising	___ Critical	___ Crafty	___ Changeable

Personality Scoring Sheet

Now transfer all your X's to the corresponding words on the Personality Scoring Sheet and add up your totals. For example, if you checked Animated on the profile, check it on the scoring sheet. (Note: The words are in a different order on the profile and the scoring sheet.)

Strengths

Popular Sanguine	Powerful Choleric	Perfect Melancholy	Peaceful Phlegmatic
1 ___ Animated	___ Adventurous	___ Analytical	___ Adaptable
2 ___ Playful	___ Persuasive	___ Persistent	___ Peaceful
3 ___ Sociable	___ Strong-willed	___ Self-sacrificing	___ Submissive
4 ___ Convincing	___ Competitive	___ Considerate	___ Controlled
5 ___ Refreshing	___ Resourceful	___ Respectful	___ Reserved
6 ___ Spirited	___ Self-reliant	___ Sensitive	___ Satisfied
7 ___ Promoter	___ Positive	___ Planner	___ Patient
8 ___ Spontaneous	___ Sure	___ Scheduled	___ Shy
9 ___ Optimistic	___ Outspoken	___ Orderly	___ Obliging
10 ___ Funny	___ Forceful	___ Faithful	___ Friendly
11 ___ Delightful	___ Daring	___ Detailed	___ Diplomatic
12 ___ Cheerful	___ Confident	___ Cultured	___ Consistent
13 ___ Inspiring	___ Independent	___ Idealistic	___ Inoffensive
14 ___ Demonstrative	___ Decisive	___ Deep	___ Dry humor
15 ___ Mixes easily	___ Mover	___ Musical	___ Mediator
16 ___ Talker	___ Tenacious	___ Thoughtful	___ Tolerant
17 ___ Lively	___ Leader	___ Loyal	___ Listener
18 ___ Cute	___ Chief	___ Chartmaker	___ Contented
19 ___ Popular	___ Productive	___ Perfectionist	___ Pleasant
20 ___ Bouncy	___ Bold	___ Behaved	___ Balanced

Totals—Strengths

_____   _____   _____   _____

Weaknesses

Popular Sanguine	Powerful Choleric	Perfect Melancholy	Peaceful Phlegmatic
21 ___ Brassy	___ Bossy	___ Bashful	___ Blank
22 ___ Undisciplined	___ Unsympathetic	___ Unforgiving	___ Unenthusiastic
23 ___ Repetitious	___ Resistant	___ Resentful	___ Reticent
24 ___ Forgetful	___ Frank	___ Fussy	___ Fearful
25 ___ Interrupts	___ Impatient	___ Insecure	___ Indecisive
26 ___ Unpredictable	___ Unaffectionate	___ Unpopular	___ Uninvolved
27 ___ Haphazard	___ Headstrong	___ Hard to please	___ Hesitant
28 ___ Permissive	___ Proud	___ Pessimistic	___ Plain
29 ___ Angered easily	___ Argumentative	___ Alienated	___ Aimless
30 ___ Naive	___ Nervy	___ Negative attitude	___ Nonchalant
31 ___ Wants credit	___ Workaholic	___ Withdrawn	___ Worrier
32 ___ Talkative	___ Tactless	___ Too sensitive	___ Timid
33 ___ Disorganized	___ Domineering	___ Depressed	___ Doubtful
34 ___ Inconsistent	___ Intolerant	___ Introvert	___ Indifferent
35 ___ Messy	___ Manipulative	___ Moody	___ Mumbles
36 ___ Show-off	___ Stubborn	___ Skeptical	___ Slow
37 ___ Loud	___ Lord over others	___ Loner	___ Lazy
38 ___ Scatterbrained	___ Short-tempered	___ Suspicious	___ Sluggish
39 ___ Restless	___ Rash	___ Revengeful	___ Reluctant
40 ___ Changeable	___ Crafty	___ Critical	___ Compromising

Totals—Weaknesses

_____   _____   _____   _____

Combined Totals

_____   _____   _____   _____

The Personality Profile is from *After Every Wedding Comes a Marriage* by Florence Littauer. Copyright © 1981, Harvest House Publishers. Used by Permission.

This test is very easy to interpret. Once you've transferred your answers to the scoring sheet, added up your total number of answers in each of the four columns, and added your totals from both the strengths and weaknesses sections, you'll know your dominant personality type. You'll also know what combination you are. If, for example, your score is 15 in Powerful Choleric strengths and weaknesses, there's really little question. You're almost all Powerful Choleric. But if your score is, for example, 8 in Popular Sanguine, 6 in Perfect Melancholy, and 2 in each of the others, you're a Popular Sanguine with a strong Perfect Melancholy. You'll also, of course, know your least dominant type.

As you read the following pages and work with the material in this book, you'll learn how to put your strengths to work for you, how to compensate for the weaknesses in your dominant type, and how to understand the strengths and weaknesses of other types.

PART TWO

Personality Potential

A Look at Our Individual Assets

You've taken the test. Now you know what personality or combination you are. Following are the strengths of each summarized. Bet you didn't know you had all this going for you! Now that you know your particular assets—make them work for you.

Popular Sanguine Personality

The Extrovert • The Talker • The Optimist

STRENGTHS

POPULAR SANGUINE'S EMOTIONS

Appealing personality
Talkative, storyteller
Life of the party
Good sense of humor
Memory for color
Physically holds on to listener
Emotional and demonstrative
Enthusiastic and expressive
Cheerful and bubbling over
Curious
Good on stage
Wide-eyed and innocent
Lives in the present
Changeable disposition
Sincere at heart
Always a child

POPULAR SANGUINE AS A PARENT

Makes home fun
Is liked by children's friends
Turns disaster into humor
Is the circus master

POPULAR SANGUINE AT WORK

Volunteers for jobs
Thinks up new activities
Looks great on the surface
Creative and colorful
Has energy and enthusiasm
Starts in a flashy way
Inspires others to join
Charms others to work

POPULAR SANGUINE AS A FRIEND

Makes friends easily
Loves people
Thrives on compliments
Seems exciting
Envied by others
Doesn't hold grudges
Apologizes quickly
Prevents dull moments
Likes spontaneous activities

Perfect Melancholy Personality

The Introvert • The Thinker • The Pessimist

STRENGTHS

PERFECT MELANCHOLY'S EMOTIONS

Deep and thoughtful
Analytical
Serious and purposeful
Genius prone
Talented and creative
Artistic or musical
Philosophical and poetic
Appreciative of beauty
Sensitive to others
Self-sacrificing
Conscientious
Idealistic

PERFECT MELANCHOLY AS A PARENT

Sets high standards
Wants everything done right
Keeps home in good order
Picks up after children
Sacrifices own will for others
Encourages scholarship and
    talent

PERFECT MELANCHOLY AT WORK

Schedule oriented
Perfectionist, high standards
Detail conscious
Persistent and thorough
Orderly and organized
Neat and tidy
Economical
Sees the problems
Finds creative solutions
Needs to finish what is started
Likes charts, graphs, figures,
    lists

PERFECT MELANCHOLY AS A FRIEND

Makes friends cautiously
Content to stay in background
Avoids causing attention
Faithful and devoted
Will listen to complaints
Can solve others' problems
Deep concern for other people
Moved to tears with compassion
Seeks ideal mate

Powerful Choleric Personality

The Extrovert • The Doer • The Optimist

STRENGTHS

POWERFUL CHOLERIC'S EMOTIONS

Born leader
Dynamic and active
Compulsive need for change
Must correct wrongs
Strong willed and decisive
Unemotional
Not easily discouraged
Independent and self-sufficient
Exudes confidence
Can run anything

POWERFUL CHOLERIC AS A PARENT

Exerts sound leadership
Establishes goals
Motivates family to action
Knows the right answer
Organizes household

POWERFUL CHOLERIC AT WORK

Goal oriented
Sees the whole picture
Organizes well
Seeks practical solutions
Moves quickly to action
Delegates work
Insists on production
Makes the goal
Stimulates activity
Thrives on opposition

POWERFUL CHOLERIC AS A FRIEND

Has little need for friends
Will work for group activity
Will lead and organize
Is usually right
Excels in emergencies

Peaceful Phlegmatic Personality

The Introvert • The Watcher • The Pessimist

STRENGTHS

PEACEFUL PHLEGMATIC'S EMOTIONS

Low-key personality
Easygoing and relaxed
Calm, cool, and collected
Patient, well balanced
Consistent life
Quiet but witty
Sympathetic and kind
Keeps emotions hidden
Happily reconciled to life
All-purpose person

PEACEFUL PHLEGMATIC AS A PARENT

Makes a good parent
Takes time for the children
Is not in a hurry
Can take the good with the bad
Doesn't get upset easily

PEACEFUL PHLEGMATIC AT WORK

Competent and steady
Peaceful and agreeable
Has administrative ability
Mediates problems
Avoids conflicts
Good under pressure
Finds the easy way

PEACEFUL PHLEGMATIC AS A FRIEND

Easy to get along with
Pleasant and enjoyable
Inoffensive
Good listener
Dry sense of humor
Enjoys watching people
Has many friends
Has compassion and concern

For further information on the personalities at work read
Personality Puzzle, by Florence and Marita Littauer
(Revell, 1992).

CHAPTER **3**

Let's Have Fun with Popular Sanguine

Oh, how this world needs Popular Sanguines!

The lift of joy in times of trouble.
The touch of innocence in a jaded era.
The word of wit when we're weighted down.
The lift of humor when we're heavyhearted.
The ray of hope to blow away our black clouds.
The enthusiasm and energy to start over and over again.
The creativity and charm to color a drab day.
The simplicity of a child in complex situations.

Popular Sanguine is off swinging on a star, bringing moonbeams home in a jar. Popular Sanguine loves the fairy tales of life and wants to live happily ever after.

The typical Popular Sanguines are emotional and demonstrative, they make work into fun, and they all love to be with people. Popular Sanguines see excitement in each experience and repeat the flavor of each occasion in colorful descriptions. Popular Sanguines are outgoing and optimistic.

One day as I was driving down the freeway with my Perfect Melancholy son, Fred, I noticed all the bankings were covered with bright, white daisies. "Look at those beautiful flowers!" I exclaimed. As Fred turned, his eyes fell on a large weed, and he sighed, "Yes, but look at that weed." He thought for a minute and then asked, "Why is it you

always see the flowers, and I always see the weeds?" The Popular Sanguine temperament sees flowers. Popular Sanguines always expect
the best.

Popular Sanguine Children

Since we are born with our own set of temperament traits, the pattern
begins to show up very early in life. Popular Sanguines innately look
for fun and games, and from the time they are little, they are inquisi-
tive and cheerful. Popular Sanguine babies play with anything they
can find, laugh and coo, and love to be with people.

Our daughter Marita is a Popular Sanguine, and she has had a
delightful sense of humor right from the beginning. Her big, bright
eyes twinkled the minute they opened. Recently, as we lined up her
yearly baby and school pictures, we could all see that consistent, imp-
ish look that has often gotten her into trouble but has made her a joy
to live with. Marita's mouth was always going, and she had an abundance of creative talent. She colored everything she could find, including the walls. When we moved from Connecticut, I wanted to bring
the basement wall along with me, because it was decorated with little
blue handprints Marita made after spilling a bottle of poster paint on
the floor. Today Marita is a media publicist, an author, and a sparkling
speaker.

Appealing Personality

Popular Sanguines may not have more talent or opportunity than other
temperaments, but they always seem to have more fun. Their bubbly
personalities and natural charisma draw people to them. Popular Sanguine children have flocks of little fans following them around, because
they want to be where the action is. As a child, our daughter Marita
always had something exciting going on. While others just played with
toy cars, she built an entire city on the side of our hill. Under her direction, she and her friends shaped streets and leveled lots. Her first building was a bank stocked with Monopoly money. To get in on the action
each child had to put up a *real* dollar to buy shares in the bank and
receive *phony* money. With the dollars, she bought plastic bricks and

equipment and sold these to others to build their homes. Each lot had a different price, according to its location in town, and those with the most money had the best sites.

Children were clambering up and down our hill all the time. I didn't know real money was involved until five-year-old Freddie tried to sell me a bunch of wild flowers to get enough money to "buy in." There were hills all around us, where every child could have created his own city for free, but Marita had proclaimed this one cliff "prime property," and it was the *only* place to live.

As Popular Sanguines grow up they continue to draw crowds. They become cheerleaders, have the leads in school plays, and are voted most likely to succeed. In office work they attract attention, put on parties, and decorate for Christmas. Where life is dull, they provide excitement.

As mothers, Popular Sanguines make the home fun and magnetize children like the Pied Piper. Since Popular Sanguines sparkle brighter in proportion to the size of the crowd, they tend to save their best for an appropriate audience. They would far rather read a story dramatically to a roomful of children than share it quietly with their own little ones.

A girl named Mary Alice told me at a seminar that she had become the hit of the neighborhood—in fact, the city—when she had found that for fifty-two dollars she could buy four hundred balloons and a tank of helium. She had a birthday party for her child, and all the little guests took turns filling balloons and letting them float away. By the time four hundred balloons were drifting over Downey, her party was the talk of the town.

Popular Sanguines' exciting activities sometimes get out of hand, however. One creative mother told me how popular she was with the neighborhood children because she always kept something special going on at her house. One day she told all the visiting children there were elephants in the backyard, and that they should hide. The doorbell rang, and the mother crawled to the door to answer. She opened at eye level with a little girl who asked her why she was crawling. "It's because the backyard is full of elephants, and I don't want them to see me. You'd better duck down yourself." The children stayed quiet and huddled, while the mother crept frequently to the window to check the elephants. At five o'clock she announced, "The elephants are all gone now, so you can go home safely."

She found out later that one little girl went home and told her mother, "Mrs. Smith had to crawl around the house all afternoon, because the backyard was full of elephants." The mother punished the child for lying.

Be cautious, Popular Sanguines, that your fun and games don't go too far.

Talkative, Storyteller

The most obvious way to spot a Popular Sanguine is by listening in on any group and locating the one who is the loudest and chatting the most constantly. While the other temperaments talk, Popular Sanguines tell stories.

When we lived in New Haven, Connecticut, the city built a seven-story parking garage. One day before Christmas, I parked my car in this gray cement structure that looked somewhat like an open penitentiary and went off to do my shopping. Popular Sanguines, being circumstantial people with short memories, have difficulty in locating misplaced items, such as cars; and when I walked out of Macy's and faced this forbidding fortress, I had *no* idea where I'd left my car.

One good thing about a Popular Sanguine woman is that she has a helpless look and can usually attract attention. True to Popular Sanguine form, I stood staring up at the seven stories and wondered where I should start. A handsome young man walked by, noticed I was bewildered, holding an armload of bundles, and asked, "What's your trouble, honey?"

"I lost my car in this seven-story garage."

"What kind of a car is it?"

"Well, that's part of the problem. I don't know."

"You don't know what kind of a car you own?" he asked in disbelief.

"Well, we own two, and I don't know which one I drove today."

He thought for a minute and then said, "Let me see your keys, and I can narrow it down."

That was no easy request, because I had to set down all my packages and empty out my entire handbag on the curb before I found two sets of car keys. By this time, another man, seeing me on my knees in the gutter, asked, "What's the matter here?"

The first man said, "She's lost her car in the seven-story parking garage."

He asked the same question: "What kind of a car is it?"

"She doesn't know."

"She doesn't *know*? Then how can we ever find it?"

I explained, before they both gave up, "It's either a yellow convertible with black insides and red dials, or a large, navy blue car with matching velour seats."

They both shook their heads, picked up my packages, and led me off to the parking garage. As we searched seven stories, other helpful souls attached themselves to our group, and we became acquainted. By the time we found the yellow convertible with the license plate O FLO we were such good buddies, I wanted to start a club and be president.

I rushed right home, eager to tell Fred every detail of my marvelous moments of hide-and-seek in the garage. Fifteen beautiful minutes later when I concluded my story, I hoped he would say, "Wasn't that wonderful of all those men to help my little wife." But, no. He shook his head solemnly and sighed, "I am so embarrassed to be married to a woman so stupid as to lose her car in a seven-story parking garage."

I soon learned to save my stories for those who would appreciate my sense of humor.

Life of the Party

Popular Sanguines have an inherent desire to be the center of attention, and this trait, along with their colorful stories, makes them the life of the party. When my brother Ron was a teenager and I was his high-school speech teacher, we used to rehearse key lines before going to parties. I'd give him reviews of current events, and he'd plot gag lines to tie in. When the subject came up in a conversation, we'd be ready with "extemporaneous" humor. As our reputation (but not our secret) got around, people bribed us—even paid us—to come to their parties.

A *Los Angeles Times* article titled "Rent a Party Guest" told of different charming and witty types people can rent to make sure their parties are successful. What a great occupation for a Popular Sanguine: going to parties each night and getting paid for doing it.

If you can't afford the luxury of rented Popular Sanguines, cultivate a few of your own and be sure to invite at least two to your dinner parties. Don't let them sit together or everyone else will feel left out. Station them at opposite ends of the table, so they won't spend the evening just amusing each other.

Memory for Color

While Popular Sanguines are not good at memorizing names, dates, places, and facts, they do have a unique ability to hold on to the colorful details of life. While they may not remember the heart of the message, they'll know the speaker wore a purple dress with a pasture of peacocks on the front and a yellow moon rising over one bosom. They may not know if they were in a church or a hall, but they'll regale you with a description of the choral director who forgot her slip and took a side stance in front of the footlights, clearly disclosing her error.

I've never had much of a memory for names, but I can hold on to colorful thoughts such as a person's occupation. When our daughter Lauren was a teenager and bringing various and assorted boyfriends through our home, I devised a creative way to remember them by making their job description their last name. It all started with David who owned a bike store and had a long name with a Z dropped somewhere in the middle of it. I can't to this day pronounce it, so I dubbed him "David Bicycle," differentiating him from "David Camera," the photographer. "Dee Plane" was a pilot and you can guess about "Don Air Force." "Bobbie Waters" worked for the water company, "Ron Loan" for the bank, and "Jeff Jobless" didn't work at all. Lauren married "Randy Coin," a numismatist, and now has little pennies of her own.

Marita followed the pattern by bringing home from the produce department of the grocery store "Jimmy Vegetable," followed by "Paul

Police." "Peter Painter" owned a paint company, and "Manny Money" was rich.

Only Popular Sanguines can take the weakness of a poor memory and turn it into a family tradition.

Hold On to the Listener

Because Popular Sanguines are very warm and physical people, they tend to hug, kiss, pat, and stroke their friends. This contact is so natural to them, they don't even notice Perfect Melancholies backing into corners, as they approach with outstretched arms.

My daughter Marita and I are both Popular Sanguines, and we love to hug each other. Since we work together, we see each other in the office and enjoy constant contact. One day Marita went out to lunch with a friend and later went shopping in Harris's, our local department store. In midafternoon, I went over to Harris's and saw Marita at the makeup counter. My natural reaction was to call, "Marita, my love!" She ran toward me, crying, "Mother Dove." We grabbed each other as long-lost friends, and kissed and hugged over the table of talcum powder. The clerk stood quietly as Marita explained, "This is my mother."

"I assumed so," she stated. "How long has it been since you've seen each other?"

Marita and I answered in unison, "A couple of hours."

"Oh, my," she gasped. "I thought it was at least a year."

Not only are Popular Sanguines "feely," but they frequently hold on to the people they are talking to in order to be in close contact and to make sure their audience doesn't get away. There is nothing that would do Popular Sanguines more psychological damage than to lose their audience before getting to the punch line.

Good on Stage

As you begin to understand the personalities, you will apply them in every area of life. The correct use of this knowledge will keep you from many mistakes and provide you with a ready feel for placing people in their proper positions. Popular Sanguines have an innate sense of the dramatic and a magnetic attraction to center stage and the lens of a camera. They gravitate to excitement and create more if the party begins to die down.

Popular Sanguines make excellent greeters, hosts, receptionists, masters of ceremony, and club presidents. They can be hilarious and arouse enthusiasm in all but the dullest of hearts. Give Popular Sanguines an audience and they'll start a script.

Wide-Eyed and Innocent

Popular Sanguine is the one personality that always appears to be wide-eyed and innocent. Popular Sanguines are naive and have childlike simplicity into old age. They aren't really dumber than other temperaments; they just sometimes look that way.

I have a friend Patti who is a perfect example. She has huge, brown eyes, and to show them up even more, she tops them with sweeping false eyelashes. She always looks as if she's standing around under a pair of awnings. Whatever you tell Patti, she bats her lashes and responds, "Why, I never ever thought of that!"

One day my husband asked me, "Hasn't Patti ever heard of anything?" For Popular Sanguine everything is a fresh thought.

Enthusiastic and Expressive

Popular Sanguines are emotional and demonstrative people who are optimistic and enthusiastic over almost everything. Whatever you bring up, they want to do, and wherever you mention going, they want to go. They move, jump, wave, and wiggle. A Popular Sanguine pastor I know often gets so excited over his sermon that he feels encumbered with one hand holding the Bible and only one free for waving, so he rises up and down on his toes and makes emphatic points with a kick of one foot. If you don't happen to be fascinated with his subject matter, you will be enthralled watching to see how long he can do this jig without losing his balance.

One girl described her Popular Sanguine family by saying, "We grew up in a house where emotions were dripping off the wall."

My friend Connie owns several beauty shops, and she told me she tries to hire Popular Sanguine hairdressers, because they are the only ones who can keep enthusiastic while listening to all the depressing problems of the patrons all day. "By afternoon their stations are a mess, the rollers are all over the place, and they are borrowing combs from each other. But they do make it through each day in one piece, and I just hire a cleaning lady to come in each night and put the place back in order."

The word *extraordinary* must have been created to describe Popular Sanguines because their every thought and word is way beyond the ordinary and is definitely extra. Miss Piggy hit on a Popular Sanguine truth when she said in her fashion tips, "Too much is never enough."

Curious

Popular Sanguines are always curious and don't want to miss anything. At parties, if one is involved in one conversation and hears his name mentioned across the room, he will stop midsentence and turn to the new voice. Many times Popular Sanguine is like a radio on which someone is spinning the dial, tuning in and out of different stations. Popular Sanguine minds flit quickly from one conversation to another, so they will not miss a thing.

They always want to "know everything." Secrets drive them crazy. They snoop for Christmas presents, and they always find out about surprise showers.

Popular Sanguines also want to investigate anything they don't already know about. One lady told me she was having her roof reshingled and she had no idea how it was done, so she climbed up the ladder. Imagine how surprised the workers were as she appeared at the top and crawled over toward the chimney. They tried to get her to go down before she fell, but she told them she wanted to learn about roofing. One man helped her up to the chimney, where she could sit and watch. As she asked questions and gestured with enthusiasm, she leaned back, lost her balance, and fell into the chimney. She screamed and the men scrambled to rescue her. It took four men to pull her out, one on each foot and hand. She had scraped her whole back on the bricks, and her white pants were covered with soot. As the men helped her over to the ladder, one said, "We don't need your Mary Poppins act up here."

Always a Child

One reason Popular Sanguines keep childlike ways is that they were such adorable children. They were doted upon by parents and teachers, and they don't want to leave this "center of attention" life. Another reason is that they don't really want to grow up. While other temperaments desire to leave childhood behind, the Popular Sanguine likes the world of make-believe. The girls are all Cinderellas and the boys are Prince Charmings. In the stories, Prince Charmings never work. They ride off into the sunset on white chargers, but they never have to go look for a job. Age brings responsibility, and Popular Sanguines innately would rather avoid settling down in life as long as possible.

Volunteers for Jobs

Since Popular Sanguines want to be helpful and popular, they volunteer without any thought of the consequences. One night at a party, Linda and Vonice were discussing their baby-sitting problems. Linda needed suggestions for an all-night sitter for her five children. Popular Sanguine Vonice said, "Don't worry, Linda, *we* will find you someone." As the time of the occasion drew near, Linda called Vonice to see how *we* were doing and found out Vonice had gone to Europe for a month's vacation.

Don't count on the Popular Sanguine's *we*, for *we* may not remember what *we* volunteered to do.

One night as Fred and I were teaching temperaments to a group in New York, I mentioned how Popular Sanguines volunteer and don't follow through. "For example," I said, "if a Popular Sanguine had volunteered to make the coffee for our break tonight, we would find that she had forgotten even to plug in the pot." At that point, an adorable, bright-eyed girl in the front row screamed, ran up the aisle, and disappeared into the kitchen. She was a Popular Sanguine; she had volunteered to make the coffee; she had never plugged in the pot; and we had nothing to drink that night. Popular Sanguines love to volunteer, and they mean well, but if you want coffee, you'd better plug it in yourself!

Creative and Colorful

The Popular Sanguine's mind is always thinking up new and exciting ideas. With each day come new challenges countered with creative activities. In any committee meeting it is the Popular Sanguine who dreams up the ideas, gets the vision for decorating the hall, and chooses a unique and exciting theme for the project.

When Lauren was in second grade, she told her teacher, "My mother always does special things for parties," and they chose me as Room Mother. My first major assignment was the Halloween Party, and Lauren kept reminding me she'd promised I'd do something really different.

This childlike confidence stirred my creative juices, and I began to plan a Halloween party the second-graders would never forget. Lauren scoffed at the mothers who brought in Kool-Aid and Styrofoam cups, so I planned orange-juice punch to be served in a big glass bowl, surrounded by little crystal cups. As my mind pictured this scene, I devised a floating ice ring, embedded with candy pumpkins. On the day of the party I went to the baker and picked up the custom cup-cakes with cute black cats on the tops, the special Halloween napkins, and the party hats for each child to wear. I made three gallons of bright-orange punch and put it all in an open plastic bucket, with the ice ring bobbing on the top. I set the cupcakes on one side of the car floor in the back and the bucket on the other side.

Being Popular Sanguine I was naturally running late, so I threw on the orange dress I had made for the party and backed hastily down my sloping drive. Just as I turned into the street, another car shot by, and I slammed on the brakes. As I heard what sounded like the surf at San Clemente, I knew the party was over. I looked fearfully into the back to see an ocean of orange juice with twenty-eight black cats bobbing atop the cupcakes, trying not to drown.

I arrived late and bedraggled, carrying a few packages of Kool-Aid, a box of vanilla wafers, and wearing the ice ring over my left wrist. Lauren cried throughout the party, and I was never asked to be Room Mother again!

Popular Sanguines can always come up with creative and colorful ideas, but they need some rational friends to help carry them out.

Inspires and Charms Others

Because Popular Sanguines have an abundance of energy and enthusiasm, they tend to attract and inspire others. Harry Truman once said that leadership is the ability to inspire others to work and make them enjoy doing it. This statement sums up Popular Sanguines and shows their subtle style of leadership. The effective Popular Sanguine thinks up the ideas and charms others into carrying them out to a productive conclusion. As Popular Sanguines begin to understand themselves, they realize they are starters, but they need friends who are finishers.

Popular Sanguine politicians have the gift of inspiring confidence in their constituents and then getting them to do the work. Really clever Popular Sanguines can have people begging to work for them for no pay. My brother Ron had this knack from childhood, and I recognized his ability to charm and motivate long before I'd ever heard of Popular Sanguines. Ron used his wit and charm to avoid work whenever possible. During the Korean War, Ron joined the army and was sent overseas on a huge troopship. On his first night out of San Francisco he heard an announcement: "Tomorrow morning you will all meet on deck and receive your work assignments for the remainder of the voyage."

Since Popular Sanguines avoid work at all cost, Ron began to conjure up a plan to keep from scrubbing decks. That next morning when the troops were called, Ron took a clipboard with paper and pen and stood next to the sergeant who was giving out the assignments. As the sergeant read off names and duties, "You ten for latrines, you twenty for scraping paint," Ron encouraged him and took a few notes. After all the men but Ron had been divided up into work groups, the sergeant dared speculate, "What is your job here?"

"I am in charge of the Talent Show," he replied with a voice of authority.

"I didn't know there was one planned," Sarge said in surprise.

"Oh, yes," Ron assured him. "We will have an exciting show on our last night before we dock. It will take me the whole trip to plan it. Incidentally, sir, you did a splendid job in assigning all the work. We'll see you around." With those positive words, Ron went off to spend two pleasant weeks of relaxation. As he strolled the deck, watching others scrape paint, he asked the men if they had any talent. It is amazing that men with no voice on shore became singers at sea, and Ron wrote down a list of performers on his clipboard. He gathered them all together on the final afternoon for a rehearsal, and then developed his humorous patter to hold it all together. That night every man joyfully attended. No one ever questioned his assignment, and the show was a hilarious climax to a dull trip. A few weeks later Ron received a parchment scroll from the government, honoring him as the one man on the ship who deserved recognition for lifting the morale of the troops.

Only a Popular Sanguine could spend two weeks doing nothing and be the only one to receive a commendation for having done it.

Makes Friends Easily

There are no strangers to Popular Sanguines, for on saying hello, they become your friends. While others hesitate or hold back, Popular Sanguine opens conversations with anyone available. As I stand in line at the checkout counter, invariably I start talking with someone. All I have to do is look in someone's basket, and I find topics to talk on.

One day as I stood in line with my Perfect Melancholy teenage son, I noticed the lady ahead of us had a basket full of bread. Since I felt this was beyond the ordinary, I asked her why she had so much bread. She told me she was going to a church supper, and she had been assigned to bring the bread. I asked her what church she attended, and soon we were into a deep discussion on doctrine. We both found the time profitable, and we parted friends. On the way to the car, my son Fred said, "It is so embarrassing to go to the store with you."

Typically wide-eyed and innocent I asked, "What do you mean?"

"You asked that poor lady why she had all that bread. It's none of your business why a stranger buys bread. I just won't stand in line with you anymore."

While a Popular Sanguine feels her friendly nature is an asset, someone of another temperament does not necessarily agree. One evening while out to dinner, I left Fred and another couple to go to the ladies' room. As I washed my hands, I noticed a girl sitting alone on the plastic couch. "Is there something wrong?" I asked.

She sighed and then sobbed, so I sat down beside her. She was a new bride, and she had just had a fight with her husband. I analyzed the problem, told her how to apologize, and sent her back to her mate. When I returned to my table, Fred asked what took me so long, and I explained how I made this new friend who needed help. The lady with us looked at me horror-stricken and said, "Isn't it dangerous to be friendly to strangers in the ladies' room?"

It may be to other temperaments, but a Popular Sanguine makes friends easily anywhere, even in ladies' rooms.

Seems Exciting

Since Popular Sanguines always do things with flair, they seem to be living more exciting lives than their friends. It's not that what they do is so unusual, but that their retelling of any event adds to its actuality.

A Popular Sanguine man sat next to me on a plane and started talking immediately about Hollywood personalities, giving the impression he was on close terms with the whole set.

"Wasn't it awful about Joan Crawford? *There* was a lady. What a hole this leaves in our town! When we lost Susan Hayward, I knew Hollywood was dead. The last time I was in the airport with her, she looked beautiful. I followed her through LAX and couldn't get my eyes off her gorgeous red hair. She walked like a queen! When we lose Bette Davis, we'll know it's all over!"

As he paused for a breath, I asked him if he was a Hollywood producer, and he said, "Oh, no, I wish I were; but I get to see a lot of the stars because I'm a desk clerk for American Airlines."

Here was a Popular Sanguine giving me personal pronouncements about the queens of Hollywood from his vantage point as a desk clerk. Whatever Popular Sanguines do always seems exciting, and others envy them when, in reality, they may have had fewer genuine experiences than those in awe.

Popular Sanguine has an unconscious ability to turn any simple task into a main event. One evening, as the whole family was gathered in the living room at our daughter Lauren's home, Marita decided to make popcorn. She jumped up and left for the kitchen, followed by four-year-old Randy. About ten minutes later, little Randy came running into the living room with his eyes round and bright like headlights.

"Come see the popcorn. It's shooting all over the place!"

We ran into the kitchen to see popcorn exploding like fluffy rockets out of the top of an air popper. We all grabbed bowls and tried to catch corn as it shot by. Marita had poured too much corn into the new air popper, turned it on, and left for the bathroom, leaving Randy in charge. The mistake turned into a hilarious party game, as we all chased the airborne corn, and little Randy thinks Aunt Marita's kind of corn is the only way to pop!

> *Being cheerful keeps you healthy. . . .*
> Proverbs 17:22 GNB

CHAPTER 4

Let's Get Organized with Perfect Melancholy

Oh, how the world needs Perfect Melancholy!

The depth to see into the heart and soul of life.
The artistic nature to appreciate the beauty of the world.
The talent to create a masterpiece where nothing existed before.
The ability to analyze and arrive at the proper solution.
The eye for detail while others do shoddy work.
The aim to finish what they start.
The pledge, "If it's worth doing, it's worth doing right."
The desire to "do all things decently and in order."

Before I understood the temperaments, I did not appreciate people who weren't like me. I wanted the fun-and-games approach to life, and I was too preoccupied with myself to realize my deficiencies or to want assistance. As I became self-analytical, I started to see that while I was a good front person, I didn't have much follow-through. I began to value Fred's depth, his sensitivity, his organization, his lists. I began to see the need for a true helpmate like Fred, and for Perfect Melancholy friends who could see beneath the surface of life.

Even as a baby the Perfect Melancholy appears to be thinking deeply. He is quiet, undemanding, and likes to be alone. He follows schedules right from the beginning and will respond best to a parent who is well organized. Noise and confusion will bother him, and he will not adapt

43

well to being dragged around to different places and having his routine upset.

When we adopted our son, Fred, we knew nothing about temperaments and didn't recognize his Perfect Melancholy nature. The caseworker told us he was a serious baby, that he never seemed to smile, and that at three months he appeared to be analyzing everyone who passed by. These traits have been consistent in his life. As a teenager, he was serious and reliable, and he was often annoyed by Marita's lighthearted attitude. He doesn't feel life is very funny and finds it impossible to smile in the morning. He still is introspective and analytical, and living in a family of strong extroverts has not changed his temperament pattern.

As adults Perfect Melancholies are the thinkers. They are people who are serious of purpose, dedicated to order and organization, and appreciative of beauty and intelligence. They don't dash off in search of excitement but analyze the best plan for their lives. Without Perfect Melancholies, we would have little poetry, art, literature, philosophy, or symphonies. We would be missing the culture, refinement, taste, and talent so deep within our natures. We would have fewer engineers, inventors, scientists; our ledgers might be lost and our columns wouldn't balance.

Perfect Melancholies are the soul, the mind, the spirit, the heart of humanity. Oh, how the world needs Perfect Melancholy!

Deep, Thoughtful, Analytical

Where Popular Sanguine is an extrovert, Perfect Melancholy is an introvert. Where Popular Sanguine loves to talk and throw everything out in the open, Perfect Melancholy is deep, quiet, and thoughtful. Where Popular Sanguine views life through rose-colored glasses, Perfect Melancholy is born with a pessimistic nature, and foresees problems before they happen and counts the cost before building. Perfect Melancholy always wants to get to the heart of the matter. Perfect Melancholy doesn't take things at face value, but digs into the inner truths.

While Popular Sanguine is *talking*, Powerful Choleric is *doing*, and Peaceful Phlegmatic is *watching*, Perfect Melancholy is *thinking, plan-*

ning, creating, inventing. Perfect Melancholies are willing to stick to dull routines if they can see a result in the future. The Perfect Melancholy child can sit by the hour at the piano practicing scales, perfecting techniques, whereas Popular Sanguine would run through "The Train Song" twice and chug off to play.

The inner workings of the mind are important to Perfect Melancholies, and they start in the crib to observe life around them. As children, Perfect Melancholies have toys that need to be studied, games that have to be analyzed. They like to work things with their fingers, come up with complicated answers to problems, and plan serious recreation with purpose.

In school Perfect Melancholies enjoy term papers and research projects, and they prefer to work alone because conversation only slows progress. They like topics they feel have never been investigated properly, and they respond well to a teacher who is organized and keeps the day going in a logical fashion.

My husband, Fred, as a child, was the only one of his family who liked to do dishes. He liked to analyze the procedure to do it better each time. When I first met him, he was training to be a manager in Stouffer's Restaurants in New York City, and he was making excellent use of his analytical skills. He still loved doing dishes and was the only one in his group to look forward to dish-room training. He liked going into the pandemonium of the dish room at lunchtime, instituting order out of chaos, and leading the busboys to victory!

Sometimes he carried this skill too far. Once when we were first married, he watched me doing dishes and commented, "You made forty-two unnecessary moves." I probably did, but I sure didn't want to hear about it!

One of Fred's talents Stouffer's liked the best was his ability to analyze restaurant problems and solve them quietly, with no fuss. As an aspiring young executive, he took pride in being able to stand at one end of the dining room and see every waitress's bow that wasn't tied correctly, every picture frame that was crooked, every salt and pepper that was not centered, every chair that wasn't pushed in properly. And then he would come home and with one sweep of the eye—you know the rest.

Perfect Melancholies usually find occupations and careers where their skills are applauded. They analyze life's problems and fill Think Tanks. The deep, thoughtful minds and the analytical natures are positive traits, but carried to extremes they cause Perfect Melancholy to brood over problems and to be constantly evaluating everyone else's performance. Under the watchful eye of Perfect Melancholy, others may become nervous and edgy.

Serious and Purposeful

Perfect Melancholies are serious people who set long-range goals and want to do only what has eternal purpose. Unfortunately, they usually marry those who love the fun and fluff of life and then are depressed over the trivia that excites their mates.

When our daughter Lauren was first married, she and I went shopping for houses. We didn't really care if we found one right off; it was such fun looking. Each one had at least a few major flaws, and by midafternoon I could hardly wait to tell Fred about the terrible structures we'd seen. I marched into his business office and sat down to regale him with the colorful stories I'd collected that very day. As I went on and on with fascinating details, Fred asked the fateful question designed to cut to the heart of the matter and bring my trivia to a stop: "Did Lauren buy a house?"

I didn't want to answer that because I would no longer be able, in good conscience, to continue my account.

"Well . . ."

"Did they buy a house?"

"No, but . . ."

"No, 'no buts.' I do not have time in my busy day to hear lengthy descriptions of all the houses they did not buy."

I went home, realizing a Perfect Melancholy doesn't need to hear an hour of trivia when the simple truth is *no*.

Genius—Intellect

Aristotle said, "All men of Genius are of Melancholy temperament." The writers, artists, and musicians are usually Perfect Melancholies because they are born with genius potential that, properly motivated and cultivated, will produce giants. Michelangelo was undoubtedly a Perfect Melancholy, although he is no longer around to take one of our tests.

Before he carved his classic statues of Moses, David, and the Pieta, he made an intensive study of the human body. He went to the morgues and personally cut up the cadavers to study the muscles and sinews. Because he went deeper into the heart of man than the average sculptor of his day, his creations have been protected and respected to this day.

Had I been led to carve a statue, I would have hacked the marble with vigor and quickly chipped away everything that didn't look like David. With luck, my creation might have been used to fill a temporary gap in front of the Point Mugu Post Office, but the Pieta adorns Saint Peter's Basilica today.

Michelangelo was also an architect; he wrote poetry, and he is best known for the frescoes on the ceiling of the Sistine Chapel in the Vatican at Rome. These nine scenes from the Book of Genesis took him four years (1508–1512) to complete while lying on his back seventy feet above the ground.

Can you imagine what would have happened if Michelangelo had been a Popular Sanguine? He would have had no plan and would have started at one corner, just painting whatever came into his mind at the moment. After he had climbed up the scaffolding, he would have found he had forgotten his red paint and had to go down again. After he had been up there alone for a few days, he would have lost interest in the whole project and quit, leaving Adam with nary a fig leaf. But Michelangelo was Perfect Melancholy, and he is remembered today as one of the greatest creative geniuses of all time.

If you are Perfect Melancholy, are you doing the very best you can to develop your innate abilities?

Talented and Creative

Perfect Melancholies are the most talented and creative of them all. They may be artistic, musical, philosophical, poetic, literary. They appreciate gifted people, admire geniuses, and admit an occasional tear of emotion. They are moved by the greats of all mediums, and they marvel at the wonders of nature. They sink into symphonies and get wired on their woofers. The more Perfect Melancholy they are, the more stereo components they need.

At a recent seminar, as we divided the people into temperament groups, Fred decided to see how many of the Perfect Melancholy group were musical. He asked the leader to count up the musical people in the room and report to us all later. When the chairman came back, he said:

> Our first problem was to define *musical*. Some of us felt it meant having musical talent, and others thought it should include those who appreciate music. We analyzed this for a while, and then decided to take two votes: one for appreciation and one for talent. I asked how many appreciated music and eighteen raised their hands. As I went to write this down, one young man asked, "Do you have to appreciate classical music or could you like contemporary?" There was no meeting of the minds on this, so we took two more counts: those who appreciated classical music and those who liked anything.
>
> Then we went back to the other part, and I asked how many had musical talent. Fifteen raised their hands, but we were interrupted by a lady who asked, "Do you have to play an instrument now? I used to play the clarinet in high school." Intense discussion followed, as we tried to determine the proper answer. No sooner had we decided to take another count, those who used to play and those who do now, when a man asked, "What if you're going to start piano lessons tomorrow?" At that our time was up, and I resigned!

Had we given this assignment to a group of Popular Sanguines, they would have forgotten the question. A Powerful Choleric chairman would have asked, "How many of you guys are musical?" and quickly counted the hands. The Peaceful Phlegmatic would have said, "What difference does it make?" Only Perfect Melancholies could take fifteen minutes defining music and come up with a five-part report.

Likes Lists, Charts, Graphs, and Figures

All of us make lists once in a while but to Perfect Melancholy the use of lists, charts, and graphs is an important part of life. Perfect Melancholy minds think in such an orderly fashion that they see figures when Popular Sanguines see people; they think in columns when Popular Sanguines think in events.

Vivian told me she loves charts and graphs and thinks everyone would love them if they only understood them. She spends time explaining the theory behind them to others and can't understand that some just don't get interested. Once she heard about the temperaments, she began to see why three-fourths of the people didn't get too excited over the best of graphs and the most colorful of charts.

While getting organized would help everyone achieve a higher level, for Perfect Melancholy it is the basic essential of life. Fred carries in his shirt pocket a packet of three-by-five-inch cards to keep himself in line. These cards are updated daily and crossed off when specific chores are completed. He also carries, clipped to the same pocket, six different types of pens. In his jacket pocket he adds three pencils and a pen with a built-in flashlight, which has come in handy for reading menus in dimly lit restaurants or finding dropped items in dark theaters. In his pants' right front pocket he always has a penknife and his change, and in his front left, a nail clipper. The handkerchief is in the right rear and his wallet is in the left rear. When he sets out in the morning, he is prepared, though bulgy.

Barbara from Detroit told me she put on a "perfect home wedding" for her daughter. She spent months charting out the whole production and had typed instructions for every member of the family, explaining their personal responsibilities. She taped the doorbell, so no one could ring it, and put a sign on the door: WEDDING IN PROGRESS. She unplugged all the phones and posted a detailed time chart for the head usher. Among other duties, he was to turn off the air conditioner on the first note of the wedding march, so the fans would not make a distracting noise. At the top of the winding staircase, Barbara tacked up the last instruction for the bride, a big sign that said SMILE!

Detail Conscious

Many of the little things in life that I don't even note are very important to Perfect Melancholies. Take the toilet paper for example. I used to put it on the roller whatever way it happened to go, until Fred pointed out I was doing it wrong. "What do you mean wrong?" I countered. "It's stayed up there, hasn't it?"

He sighed, "Yes, it's stayed up but it's on wrong. You have it backward."

Even staring, I couldn't see how toilet paper could be backward, but he showed me that the paper should come off the front of the roll—not hang down the back against the wall where you would have to go hunting for it. I didn't think you had to hunt far, but I agreed to do it his way and worked at remembering.

Years later, when printed toilet paper came out, Fred was so excited to show me how the little flowers blossom correctly if you put the roll on right, but are looking face-to-face with the tiles if you put it on backward. I had to agree he made sense, and he felt vindicated. Now when I go into a home and the paper's on wrong, I feel compelled to take it off and reverse it.

When Fred shares this example at our seminars, I am always amazed at the number of Perfect Melancholies who come up and thank him for making it clear to their mates that there is only one right way to hang up toilet paper.

Perfect Melancholies are experts at keeping track of details, so they make excellent traveling companions for Popular Sanguines, because they are able to hang on to airline tickets, not lose the luggage, and even remember what gate the man mentioned.

Perfect Melancholies are assets on committees because they ask questions about details overlooked by Popular Sanguines, such as *Can we afford this project? How much will it cost to rent the hall? How many people do you think will come? How much are you going to charge? Is there a demand for this activity? Do you realize the dates you've chosen are on Easter weekend?* Without Perfect Melancholy balance, many committees would go wild with enthusiasm without counting the cost.

Orderly and Organized

While Popular Sanguine is seeking fun in life, Perfect Melancholy is in pursuit of order. Popular Sanguines can function in a messy kitchen or work on a cluttered desk, but Perfect Melancholies must have things organized, or they can't function.

A young girl told me she was helping a lady clean her house as an after-school job. She finished her work and returned all the bottles to the cabinet. As she turned to leave, the lady called her back to tell her she had not put things away properly. The girl gasped as the lady showed her circles drawn on the shelf paper to indicate exactly where each can or bottle went—round for Ajax, oval for Windex, rectangle for detergent, big round for bleach. She placed everything on its own space and said, "When you keep things in perfect order, you can always put your hands on them quickly."

Perfect Melancholies love organized, orderly closets. Fred has sections for short-sleeved shirts, knit shirts, and dress shirts. His pants each have their own hanger and their own belt, so he will never pull two pants off while reaching for one, or have to hunt for the appropriate belt in a hurry. His jackets and pants are hung in rotating order. When he takes them off at night, they go on the left side of their section, and the next day he chooses from the right. This system ensures variety of style and evenness of wear. His shoes are in neat rows on the closet floor, and he does a thorough polishing job on them all once a month.

When we were first married I would fold Fred's laundry Popular Sanguine style and felt if it fit in and you could still shut the drawer, you had a victory. One day Fred said, "I appreciate your doing my laundry, but I wish you'd leave it all out on the dresser and let me put it away." When I asked my frequent question, "What am I doing wrong?" he showed me how I rolled up his socks and just threw them in the drawer. He then folded each sock correctly in half and piled them with the heels heading in the same direction. By the time he finished this arrangement, the contents of his drawers fit together like a jigsaw puzzle.

In almost forty years I've never quite mastered the Perfect Melancholy art of fastidious folding and am rather fascinated with a rollicking romp through a stuffed drawer where the joy of discovery is half the fun!

The Perfect Melancholy wife of a doctor developed a double file system for her social entertaining. One file box had the cards under the occasion, such as CHRISTMAS 1975, EASTER 1980, and listed all who attended, plus the menu. The other box held cards, alphabetized by names of every guest. Each card gave the date of each time the person had come, the guest's reaction to the menu (if any comments were made), and a column to check off if the guest had sent a thank-you note. On the back was a record of when she had been invited to that person's house. She knew every detail of every dinner party for fourteen years.

For those of us who are not of this temperament, it is necessary for us to realize how important organization and order are to Perfect Melancholy, and how much it would help each one of us to at least head in this direction.

Neat and Tidy

Perfect Melancholy is usually well dressed and meticulously groomed. The male looks efficient, and the female has every hair in place. They want their surroundings to be neat and tidy, and they go around picking up after others. When Fred and I went to Europe fifteen years ago, we had in our group two loud Popular Sanguine ladies whose sole interest in museums and cathedrals was getting their pictures taken in front of them. They had a suitcase full of Polaroid film, and while the rest of us were listening to the tour guide prepare us for the Parthenon, they were posing by the pillars on the portico. As they pulled out the black innards of their Polaroid, they would drop them wherever they were and go off to a new location. Fred's sense of neatness would not allow the ugly Americans to leave a trail of sticky black paper through Europe, so he followed behind them for two weeks and cleaned up the castles. Once he tried to show them their folly by quietly handing one lady her debris.

"Pardon me, but you dropped this."

She replied, "Oh, that's all right. It's not worth anything."

Young Fred has exhibited Perfect Melancholy traits from the time he was a baby and analyzed us through the bars of his crib. As a toddler, he played neatly with his toys and lined his trucks all up before he took his nap. As soon as he could make his bed, he made sure the big awning stripes on his spread were in perfect lines, even with the edge. He placed each stuffed toy in the same spot against the pillow each day, and if anyone moved one item, he knew it.

One Perfect Melancholy young man told me he had a date with a Popular Sanguine girl. He went to her office to pick her up on time. He was appalled at the condition of her desk and also at the fact she had gone on an errand and didn't seem to remember their engagement. As he sat, waiting, he noticed the desk next to hers was meticulous. The desk calendar had neat entries; the pencils were lying with their sharpened points in one direction; and the IN and OUT baskets were empty. The girl with the prize desk came in, and he began to talk with her. She was dressed attractively and seemed to know what she was doing.

"Suddenly," he said, "I could see I was after the wrong girl. The first one never showed up anyway, so I took the second to lunch, and we've been dating—in an orderly fashion—ever since."

Perfectionist—High Standards

Perfect Melancholy's motto in life is *If it's worth doing, it's worth doing right.* It's never a matter of how fast he can do it, but how well. The quality is always more important than the quantity, and when a Perfect Melancholy is in charge, you know the job will be done correctly and on time.

Cindy told me her Perfect Melancholy husband, Phil, wanted their house painted, but he knew only he could do it right. He started by sanding down every shingle by hand. This job took him one full year, during which time the house looked extremely shabby. At the end of the year, he had painted it meticulously, but he was transferred and they sold the house. She did admit they got a higher price because of the perfect paint job.

Our Perfect Melancholy paperboy showed me a handful of crumpled dollar bills he had and told me he always ironed them all flat before he turned them in because he hated wrinkled money. Only a Perfect Melancholy would steam press his money.

While I feel I am a neat housekeeper, my Perfect Melancholy son, Fred, does not think I am up to his standards. One time when Marita and I went off on a trip, Fred sighed with relief. He looked up at his father and said, "Now that the girls are gone, I'll be able to get this house into shape and keep it that way." During the first evening he vacuumed the floors, polished the living-room furniture, and rearranged the figurines in straight Perfect Melancholy rows on the shelves.

In a day and age where mediocrity is accepted as above average, Perfect Melancholy shines as a beacon of high standards for the rest of us to follow.

Economical

Perfect Melancholies by nature cannot be wasteful, and they love to get a bargain. Fred cuts the money-saving coupons out of the paper neatly with scissors and saves them for the right moment. If I do it at all, I rip them out and arrive in the store with these odd, shaggy papers. Fred's big moment in life is when he has a coupon worth a dollar off on a pound of coffee, and the supermarket has Double Coupon Days. Once there was also a double coupon in the can, and he was euphoric at actually being paid thirty-seven cents to drink the coffee. Popular Sanguines never send those rebate coupons in, but Perfect Melancholies make sure they get everything they deserve.

Fred not only shops for bargains, but he checks the trash to make sure I don't throw away anything of value. He will decide a mayonnaise jar could be useful if I'd wash it; that the bananas I've tossed would be just fine in banana bread; and that there are still a few good sweeps in the old broom. If I want to make sure he doesn't scrounge something up, I have to take it next door and hide it in the neighbor's trash.

My grandmother used to save string, and she had one jar of ends labeled STRING TOO SHORT TO USE. One Perfect Melancholy lady I know puts every little leftover in a plastic container in the refrigerator. She writes on the top the name of the item and the date she put it away. She puts today's entry in the back, pushing the other jars to the front. This way she eats the leftovers in order, and nothing ever goes to waste.

Deep Concern and Compassion

Perfect Melancholy has true concerns for other people and is sensitive to their needs. While Popular Sanguine is trying to be the center of attention, Perfect Melancholy is observing others and is compassionate over their problems. A sweet Perfect Melancholy friend told me she had been moved to tears as she watched a whole plane load of Vietnam orphans on TV. As her heart went out to them, her Powerful Choleric husband asked, "What in the world are you crying for? You don't know one of them!"

When we go to a parade, Fred is touched by the sight of Old Glory as it passes by and is stirred by the thoughts of all our American men who have died for their country. At the same time, I'm scanning the crowd for a familiar face and hoping to pull a party together for after the parade.

Perfect Melancholies make excellent counselors because they have a deep ability to see into the hearts of others. They are willing to listen to people's problems, analyze them, and come up with viable solutions. Popular Sanguines can't keep still long enough to hear someone's troubles, and they don't like to get involved in anything negative, but Perfect Melancholy has sincere compassion for others and really cares.

Seeks Ideal Mate

Because Perfect Melancholies are perfectionists, they want perfect mates. They make friends cautiously, to see if people measure up, and they would rather have a few faithful, devoted friends than an abundance of acquaintances as do Popular Sanguines.

Before deciding to propose to me, Fred made a chart of all the attributes he wanted in a wife. He checked me off on all these points and found I came out to be about 90 percent of what he wanted. He figured he had the rest of his life to shape up the other 10 percent. But what happened after we got married? The little faults became magnified, and the things that were missing became necessities.

After a while Fred became depressed at how poorly I was doing and, when he told me about the chart, I was stunned that he had plotted me out on a graph—and even more upset that he felt I had failed. If we had only known the temperaments at that point, I could have understood his charts and desire for perfection, and he could have realized his standards were too high for a Popular Sanguine. We both could have been spared these and many other problems.

As we shared this story at a seminar in Whittier, a strikingly beautiful young girl came up to talk with us. She had, years before, made a list of twelve characteristics for a perfect husband and had used this to measure her dates. The best young man had nine, and she had been engaged to him for seven years, waiting for him to improve. We suggested she either learn to accept him as he was or set him free, so he could find a girl with a list of nine or less. She let us know later she had broken her engagement. Seeking ideals in life is a positive goal, but we have to realize we will never find perfect people.

Perfect Melancholy is idealistic, organized, and purposeful.

A sensible man watches for problems ahead and prepares to meet them. The simpleton never looks, and suffers the consequences.

Proverbs 27:12 TLB

CHAPTER **5**

Let's Look at
Our Emotions

Time out! (for a few minutes of reflection)

By now I'm sure you all have an understanding of the bubbly, cheerful Popular Sanguine and the deep, analytical Perfect Melancholy. Both of these temperaments, while extremely opposite in purpose and reactions, have one major trait in common. They are both emotional and circumstantial. Popular Sanguine lives by feelings and life is a series of quick ups and downs. A typical Popular Sanguine may have had six emotional crises before noon. Everything is either great or terrible—no middle ground. The Popular Sanguine mother can be talking joyfully on the phone when her child falls off a chair. She screams, "He's killed himself!" and drops the phone. She grabs the child up and runs through the house, screaming along with him, looking for Band-Aids. The doorbell rings, and it's the pastor who's come to call. She lets him in, rushes the child to his crib, throws him a towel to mop up the blood and says, "Don't you dare cry; that's the pastor." She sweeps into the living room with a smile and says sweetly, "Isn't it a beautiful day!"

Can you sense the emotional toll this kind of life takes on a Popular Sanguine? If you were to chart out a Popular Sanguine's emotions on a graph, they would go up and down, up and down. . . .

Perfect Melancholy stands back and observes this frenzied life with critical judgment. "If only she'd calm down." "If only he'd get himself pulled together."

Prolonged Pattern

What Perfect Melancholies don't realize is that they are also emotional, except their highs are higher, their lows lower, and the whole pattern is prolonged. Let's say Perfect Melancholy is at a normal middle-of-the-mood point. Nothing has bothered him yet. He reaches for his lunch bag, and his Popular Sanguine wife has forgotten to make him a sandwich. He calls to her and watches while she tears around, throwing it together. She licks her fingers off as she's poking the lettuce in, and he thinks, *How unsanitary!* but of course he's not emotional like her, so he keeps quiet. She picks the sandwich up and pulls out the drawer where she keeps the Baggies. It sticks, and she yanks at it. This throws her backward across the kitchen, and she drops the sandwich. He watches as she picks the parts up from the floor and piles them back together saying, "A little dirt never hurt anyone." By this time Perfect Melancholy's stomach is in a knot, and he wishes he'd thought of going to McDonald's.

He leaves home smoldering, but calm. The next day she forgets again, and he calls her, but starts to make a sandwich himself. The liverwurst is moldy and the bread is dry, because she didn't wrap it properly. He points this out clearly to her, and she bursts into tears. She's so emotional and unstable.

The third day he makes the sandwich himself. He has brought home the right ingredients, and he fumes, as he hears her laughing on the phone, while she should be thinking of him. He leaves without saying good-bye—and he slams the door. She needs to be jarred a little. When he comes home that night he hardly speaks, and she asks what's wrong. He says nothing, and the game goes on.

After he's been convincingly depressed for a week, she gets out of him that it's because she can't remember to make him a sandwich. She yells, "You don't speak to me for over a week over a piece of salami?"

He sinks lower into his depression and wonders why she has to be so emotional. It takes weeks of her making dutiful sandwiches before he gets back up to zero again. Do you see the pattern? They're both emotional and circumstantial. Popular Sanguine is up and down by the minute, and Perfect Melancholy is up and down by the month.

A Lot in Common

Each one sees the other one as emotional. Perfect Melancholy can prove Popular Sanguine's a nervous wreck. Popular Sanguine can't believe anyone can get so depressed over nothing. As these two begin to understand their emotional patterns, they find they have a lot in common. They are both emotional—but at a different pace. When they can begin to lay their problems in the open, they can release the tension. Perfect Melancholy can help alleviate some of the daily crises of Popular Sanguine, and Popular Sanguine, by better planning and sensitivity, can prevent the plunges of Perfect Melancholy.

Dealing with Powerful Choleric and Peaceful Phlegmatic

Where Popular Sanguine and Perfect Melancholy are emotional and circumstantial, these two are not so complex. Powerful Choleric is a direct, clear, active person with one single goal: *to get it done my way—NOW!*

Peaceful Phlegmatic is an easygoing, adaptable, all-purpose person who wants above all to avoid controversy and conflict.

Powerful Choleric may have a momentary explosion when someone doesn't do things right, but after he's put everyone in their place, he feels it's all over and he goes back to his steady drive. Peaceful Phlegmatic may have a momentary dip in his low-level line when he somehow fails to stay out of trouble, even with his firm resolve to do so, but you may not even notice it. Peaceful Phlegmatic prides himself on his stability and says, "I never let anyone know how I'm feeling about anything."

You can tell how Popular Sanguine feels as his emotions turn on and off, as if by a light switch.

You can tell the mood of Perfect Melancholy by whether or not he brought his black cloud into the room with him.

But Powerful Choleric is always on a high, dynamic course, and Peaceful Phlegmatic is hanging in there, steady and low key.

As flighty Popular Sanguine is attracted to the deep Perfect Melancholy, and withdrawn Perfect Melancholy is attracted to outgoing Popular Sanguine, so the Powerful Choleric leader loves the Peaceful Phlegmatic follower, and the Peaceful Phlegmatic indecisive nature looks for a person of decision.

As Popular Sanguine and Perfect Melancholy can fill in what's missing in each other, so will Powerful Choleric and Peaceful Phlegmatic be complementary when they begin to understand and accept each other's temperaments. As we continue to study the Powerful Choleric and Peaceful Phlegmatic temperaments, you will see what I mean.

To learn, you must want to be taught. . . .

Proverbs 12:1 TLB

Let's Get Moving with Powerful Choleric

Oh, how this world needs Powerful Choleric!

The firm control when others are losing theirs.
The cut of decision for foggy minds.
The grip of leadership to head us to the good.
The willingness to take a chance in a doubtful situation.
The confidence to hold true in the face of ridicule.
The independence to stand alone and be counted.
The road map to life when we've gone astray.
The urge to "take arms against a sea of troubles and,
    by opposing, end them."

Powerful Choleric is the dynamic person who dreams the impossible dream and aims to reach the unreachable star. He feels, like Robert Browning, "A man's reach must exceed his grasp or what's a heaven for?" Powerful Choleric is always aiming, reaching, succeeding. While Popular Sanguine is talking and Perfect Melancholy is thinking, Powerful Choleric is achieving. He is the easiest temperament to understand and get along with, as long as you live by his golden rule: "Do it *my* way NOW!"

Powerful Cholerics are similar to Popular Sanguines in that they are both outgoing and optimistic. Powerful Choleric can communicate openly with people, and he knows everything will turn out all right—as long as he's in charge. He gets more done than other temperaments, and he lets you know clearly where he stands. Because Powerful Choleric is goal oriented and has innate leadership qualities, he usually rises to the top in whatever career he chooses. The majority of our political leaders are primarily Powerful Choleric. In the early eighties, we saw two excellent examples, a man and a woman: Secretary of State Alexander Haig and Britain's Prime Minister Margaret Thatcher. In a *Time* magazine cover story (March 16, 1981), entitled "The 'Vicar' Takes Charge," George J. Church wrote:

> ... Rarely has a new Secretary of State moved so swiftly to take control of foreign policy as Alexander Meigs Haig, Jr., 56—former White House Chief of Staff in the darkest days of Watergate, former NATO commander, soldier-bureaucrat-diplomat whose self-assurance is matched only by his iron will. Said liberal Democratic Senator Paul Tsongas of Massachusetts, toward the close of Haig's confirmation hearings in January: "He will use this talent to dominate this Administration."
>
> If not, it will hardly be for lack of trying. Shortly after Reagan announced his nomination in December, Haig signaled his take-charge determination by dismissing members of the transition team that had been studying foreign policy; he consigned its uninspired reports to a shredder. Only hours after Reagan took the Inaugural oath, Haig handed Presidential Counsellor Edwin Meese a memo proposing a reorganization of foreign policy decision-making machinery that would make the Secretary of State supreme; two weeks ago, Reagan approved a directive giving Haig most, though not quite all, of the power he wanted. Faster than any other Cabinet member, Haig picked a nearly complete team of subordinates. ...

Typical Powerful Choleric words can be spotted here: *swiftly, control, commander, self-assurance, iron will, dominate, take-charge determination, consigned, reorganization, decision-making machinery, supreme, directive, power, faster, complete.*

As you begin to understand the temperaments and apply them in your everyday life, even reading *Time* magazine will be more fun, and your ability to understand other people and predict their responses will increase rapidly.

An article about Margaret Thatcher, former Prime Minister of England, also used many Powerful Choleric terms: *excelled, dominated, tal-*

ented, capable, queenly, decisively, intensely competitive, tougher, more direct,
challenged, aggressive tactics, deadly, resents suggestions. From pulling
these words out, it is easy to see that she is a Powerful Choleric leader.
She is said to "dress severely in strong colors and speak with persua-
sion." Here is a dynamic woman, exuding confidence and control.

Born Leader

Powerful Cholerics will exhibit a take-charge attitude very early in life.
They are born leaders and will look out through the bars of their cribs
and plan how soon they will take over from Mother. With them, it is
not a question of *will they take control*, but *when*. They will let their parents know what they expect out of life, they will be demanding of their
rights very early, and they will use a loud voice or temper tantrums to
solidify control.

Often when I talk with mothers who don't understand the personalities, they tell me of these strong-willed children who won't do anything they are told; who make decisions for the whole family; and who,
at an early age, are firmly in charge of the household.

Our daughter Lauren is a Powerful Choleric. From the time she
could first walk, she was mature and able to manage the household.
When Marita was born, Lauren, who was four, became a competent
second mother. She could be trusted to heat the bottle correctly, and
she trained the baby-sitters. When she was in nursery school, the
teacher told me, "I never worry about being absent, because I know
Lauren could run the whole class with no outside help." And she was
right. Lauren was a leader all through school, and got her B.A. degree
in psychology and business.

I recently visited in a home where eight-year-old Jenny was resident
queen. She had four older brothers and sisters who *moved* when she
said so. Her Powerful Choleric mother ran the family business, but
when she came home she was submissive to Jenny. "It's easier than fight-
ing her," she claimed.

At six o'clock one night the mother announced, "We are taking Mrs.
Littauer out to the steak house for dinner."

Jenny stated clearly, "I want pizza!"

Right then Jenny and I knew we were going out for pizza, but the mother had to look strong in front of me, so she repeated, while squeezing Jenny's arm for emphasis, "We *are* going out for *steak*."

Jenny pulled away with, "Don't pinch me. I want pizza." Her eyes shot daggers at her mother and the ultimate victory was clear.

Jenny threw herself on the floor and began to cry. The brothers and sisters ran in and asked, "Why is Jenny crying?"

"Because she wants to go out for pizza."

"Then why don't we go and keep her happy?"

"Well, all right. We'll go out for pizza."

At this point, Jenny jumped up quickly, winked at me in victory, and we all went out for pizza.

The next day I asked her mother, "When did Jenny first take control of the family?" The mother sighed, "When she was about three months old, I guess. She learned early that when she screamed, we all ran, and she's been bossing us around ever since."

On a trip home from Canada, Marita, who combines much Powerful Choleric with her Popular Sanguine temperament, had to fly into Spokane to transfer to Seattle, and then on to Los Angeles. When her plane landed in Spokane, she was told the flight to Seattle was unavailable (with no explanation). She walked to the proposed gate anyway, and found a group of agitated passengers and no airline personnel. She went to the next gate and got as much information as possible from the clerk. When she returned, she sat up on the high ticket counter and began doling out her limited knowledge to whoever asked. Soon people were looking to her for leadership on several subjects, including directions to the men's room.

As it became apparent the flight was going to be hours late, and there was mutiny brewing in her flock, Marita went to the Hertz counter and checked on the cost of renting cars to drive to Seattle. With all the facts in hand, she went back to her perch above the crowd and called for their attention. Everyone listened as she explained Plan B. She asked those who wanted to let Hertz put them in the driver's seat to raise their hands. She then divided them into groups of six, appointed a captain for each group to drive, and a treasurer to collect the money. As she led them off happily to Hertz, one woman said, "It's so nice of the airlines to hire a lovely girl to take care of us."

In times of crisis Powerful Choleric takes control.

Compulsive Need for Change

Powerful Cholerics are compulsive and they must change whatever they see out of place and correct whatever wrongs are being put upon the helpless. Powerful Cholerics rise quickly to causes and campaigns for the right. They are never indifferent or apathetic but concerned and confident.

Powerful Cholerics straighten pictures in other people's houses and polish the silver in restaurants. One day, when I was at a Popular Sanguine friend's home, helping her with the dishes, I noticed her silver drawer was full of crumbs and the silver was all mixed up. Without thinking of what I was doing, I dumped out all the silver, cleaned the divided tray, and sorted the pieces all out into the proper compartments. When she viewed all the forks in one section and the spoons neatly in another, she blinked and said, "Now I see why those trays have all those little sections. I never understood before."

At a Personality Plus seminar in Phoenix, my Powerful Choleric friend Marilyn and I were in the midst of an intense conversation, when her sister Mary Sue came up between us. Neither one of us missed a beat, but I noticed Mary Sue's collar was tucked under, and I automatically reached up to fix it. As I had my hand on her shoulder, I noticed Marilyn's hand on the other shoulder, brushing some lint off her jacket. Without even knowing what we were doing, we two Powerful Cholerics were compulsively correcting some little wrong.

Strong-Willed and Decisive

All organizations, businesses, and families need the strength of will and ability to make decisions that come pre-packaged in Powerful Choleric. Where others can't make up their minds, Powerful Choleric will decide instantly. They solve problems and save time, although not everyone appreciates their decisiveness.

Helen came up to me after a seminar and said, "Now I know what happened on my trip to Europe. I didn't know the temperaments then, but I obviously went on a tour with three Peaceful Phlegmatic friends." She then told me how indecisive they were, and how she had to take charge. "Each night I'd tell them what time to meet in the hotel lobby and what to wear. 'Be downstairs at 7:30 A.M. sharp, and be sure to have on your walking shoes because we'll be touring Windsor Castle.' They didn't get excited over anything, and I had to pull them off buses to get them to see the sights. One refused to go into Notre Dame because she felt all cathedrals look alike. Each afternoon when we returned, they'd want to take a nap and I'd have to remind them, 'Don't sleep too long or you'll miss the night tour.' If it hadn't been for me, they'd be standing in Piccadilly Square today! The hardest thing to take is the fact that not one of them has called me since our return."

Powerful Cholerics have a difficult role in life. They have the answers; they know what to do; they can make quick decisions; they bail others out—*but* they are rarely popular because their assurance and assertiveness make others feel insecure, and their ability to lead can easily make them appear bossy. By understanding the temperaments, Powerful Choleric should try to moderate their actions, so that others will rejoice in the Powerful Choleric's obvious abilities and not be offended by them.

Can Run Anything

Powerful Cholerics can run anything, whether or not they have any knowledge of the bylaws. In fact, I've never joined anything where I couldn't see the possibility of becoming president within the year. I once became president of the Connecticut Speech and Drama Association at the first meeting I went to—*before* I even joined. Powerful Choleric has the innate ability to rise to the top and take over.

One of the hardest disciplines I've had to put upon myself is to keep from straightening out everyone else's problems. This sounds easy to all of you, except Powerful Cholerics, who instantly run everything whether or not they've ever been to it before. Our mayor's Powerful Choleric wife and I went to a luncheon for five hundred women. They had placed the long buffet tables in a V with women coming from each end and meeting in the middle with sometimes disastrous results. Several bumped plates, spilling their food, and some dropped their dishes, which shattered on the tile floor. The line moved very slowly, and they ran out of food before our section even got into line. As I sat there, I did a Powerful Choleric appraisal of the situation and noticed Penny was deep in thought also. I asked her what she was plotting, and she came up with the exact plan I had. We both could see that the tables should have been set in an X, which would have allowed four lines to function simultaneously, and no one would come face to face with an opposing force.

We both laughed as we realized how our Powerful Choleric minds were busy straightening out the errors of others, even when the whole procedure was totally out of our hands. Powerful Cholerics naturally see the practical answers to life's problems and can't imagine why no one else has come up with the right idea.

Goal Oriented

Powerful Choleric is always more interested in achieving goals than pleasing people. This is both a positive and negative, in that they tend to end up on top alone. One Junior Women's Club president I know set unbelievable goals for what her chapter was going to achieve in her year. She motivated the troops and kept on everyone's back to make sure they were marching in step. At the end of her term, her club won more District Awards than any other, but she confessed, "I don't have a friend left in the group."

When I was president of the Women's Club of San Bernardino, I asked one Powerful Choleric lady to be a committee chairwoman, and she replied, "I'd be glad to be chairwoman if I don't have to have a committee. Those women get in the way."

Powerful Cholerics can always do the work better if they can keep the people out of the way. They frequently become loners, not by intent, but because no one can keep up with them, and they let others know that they are a hindrance to progress.

Organizes Well

Since I have the opportunity to visit in many homes, I observe how mothers of different temperaments raise their children. My friend Connie in Phoenix is a perfect Powerful Choleric who has her home running smoothly and efficiently, because of her ability to organize and her willingness to follow up on her instructions. Her two young sons, Andy, a Powerful Choleric, and Jay, a Peaceful Phlegmatic, have been so well trained that they can keep the home together, even when she is away. One evening, Marita and I arrived much later than expected, and Connie had left for a meeting. Andy met us at the door and said, "Mother had to go out, but Jay and I will get your dinner." As we watched them go about the preparations, I noticed a card on the counter with these simple instructions:

> ANDY: Fix salad, lettuce leaf, fruit mix on top.
>   Dish up soup.
> JAY: Pour ice water.
>   Warm the bread.
>
> Dessert in refrigerator. Put on mint garnishes.

Within minutes they had each fulfilled their assignments, and we enjoyed a lovely meal together. Very few boys ten and twelve could have performed so efficiently, but they had been trained by an organized and consistent mother.

As I looked around I saw that Connie had placed simple reminders to the boys in strategic spots. On the TV was a neatly printed sign, ONE HOUR OF TV ON WEEKNIGHTS, IF YOU'VE FINISHED YOUR SCHEDULE. TV ON WEEKENDS BY PERMISSION.

On the piano a three-by-five-inch card said, COUNT OUT LOUD. In the bathroom, taped to the mirror, KEEP SINK AND MIRRORS CLEAN, and in the kitchen, 25¢ IF DISHES NOT TAKEN TO SINK.

Mothers of other temperaments see this organization as too much work, but I know from experience it makes for a happy and efficient home. From the time my children were little, I trained them to help and put up a Work Chart for them to check off as they achieved their goals. I believe that when Mother stands, we all stand. When Mother works, we all work.

Because I organized and trained them well, they have grown up to be disciplined workers, even though their temperaments all differ. In any business or home situation, organization is a necessity to achieve goals. The person who doesn't know where he's going, doesn't get there. Powerful Choleric is a master at quick, practical organization.

Delegates Work

Powerful Choleric's greatest asset is his ability to accomplish more than anyone else, aided by his gift for organization. When he looks at any task, he sees instantly how it should be handled, and he divides the project into mental chunks of work. He knows what assistance he has available, and he quickly portions out the chores among the group. He is not above giving responsibilities to idle bystanders (as he assumes anyone would rather work than sit around).

As our children were growing up, Fred and I, both being part Powerful Choleric, made up Work Charts, on which we listed each child's duties for the day. When they came home from school, they checked the chart and did what was expected of them before going out to play. If any guest child stayed in our home longer than three days, I put him on the chart and assigned work. I overheard one boy say to young Fred, "Your mother must like me. She put my name on the Work Chart."

I feel so many mothers ignore the potential labor force they have free in their home, because it's too much work to set up a simple system to delegate responsibilities.

Some Powerful Cholerics are so anxious to keep tight control that they only delegate the menial tasks—the "dummy work"—and save the grand plan for themselves. Carried to extremes, this protection of control keeps them from achieving as much as they could have done had they learned to deal with people and delegate more wisely.

Thrives on Opposition

Powerful Cholerics not only like to achieve goals, but they thrive on opposition. If Popular Sanguines set out to accomplish a task, and someone says it can't be done, they thank the person profusely—and quit. Perfect Melancholies regret the time they've spent in planning and analyzing the situation, and Peaceful Phlegmatics are grateful it can't be done, because it sounded too much like work in the first place. But tell Powerful Cholerics it's impossible, and it just whets their appetite.

Lorna told me when her husband ignored a certain household task, she could get him to do it by saying, "Your mother was over today, and I told her you were going to hang these drapes and she said, 'Why Joe doesn't have any idea how to hang drapes!'" He would rise from the couch and promptly nail them to the wall.

One of the reasons so many Powerful Cholerics become professional athletes is they love the challenge of doing in the opposition. While other temperaments might be fainthearted when faced with eleven huge men on a football field, Powerful Choleric gets excited in the heat of battle. Whether male or female, Powerful Choleric has the killer instinct, the desire to beat the odds, that catapults him or her to the top in the business world today. They are not discouraged by criticism or daunted by the disinterested. They put their eye on the goal and thrive on opposition.

Has Little Need for Friends

While Popular Sanguine needs friends for an audience, and Perfect Melancholy needs friends for support, Powerful Choleric doesn't need anyone around. He has his projects, and he considers socializing a waste of time because it is not accomplishing anything. Powerful Choleric will work for group activity when it has a purpose and will be glad to jump in and organize your fund drive, but he has no need to spend time in idle chatter.

Is Usually Right

Powerful Choleric has a built-in antenna for sensing situations, and he will make a pronouncement only if he knows he's right. While this trait is a great asset, others who deal with Powerful Choleric don't always appreciate his track record. Missy once told me her Powerful Choleric husband never made a mistake, and this fact really irked her. She kept hoping he'd trip and fall to show he was human. One day the thought came to her: If she were going to hire a business manager to run her family, she would want one who didn't make any mistakes. She already had one at no charge, and from then on she looked at him in a new positive light.

Excels in Emergencies

The Powerful Choleric in me loves emergencies. One day, when I was about to speak to a Santa Rosa club, all the lights in that end of the city abruptly went out. Women shrieked and gasped as they tried to find their water glasses in a dark restaurant. Any speaker but a Powerful Choleric would have voted to close up and go home, but my mind immediately went into high gear as I planned a new approach to speaking in the dark. Lines came to me such as:

> "I've gotten to the age now where I look best in dim corners."
> "With nothing to look at, you'll have to listen."

As I plotted this new introduction to my prepared talk, the lights came on, and Santa Rosa never heard my prelude on the joys of darkness.

Another time, as I was in the middle of a message at the Shrine Auditorium in Indianapolis, a thirty-piece bagpipe band struck up "The Campbells Are Coming" right behind the stage. I was completely drowned out, and while the chairman fled to quiet the pipes, I created a new twist to my talk. Soon the notes wound down as air coming out of a tire, and the chairman announced the Shriner's Marching Band had been practicing for Saturday's parade without knowing we were only a wall away. Quickly I mentioned how appropriate it was to have a Scottish band as a musical interlude while I spoke, for my mother, Katie MacDougall, once played the bagpipes and marched in her kilts. I then finished my life story with an ethnic twist to my Scottish roots.

Oh, how Powerful Cholerics love emergencies, so they can rise to unexpected situations and lead off in new directions, especially when accompanied by a thirty-piece bagpipe band.

> *Without wise leadership, a nation is in trouble; but with good counselors there is safety.*
>
> Proverbs 11:14 TLB

CHAPTER 7

Let's Relax with Peaceful Phlegmatic

Oh, how the world needs Peaceful Phlegmatic!

The stability to stay straight on course.
The patience to put up with provokers.
The ability to listen, while others have their say.
The gift of mediation, uniting opposite forces.
The purpose of peace at almost any price.
The compassion to comfort those hurting.
The determination to keep your head, while all around are losing theirs.
The will to live in such a way that even your enemies can't find anything bad to say about you.

Understanding the personalities is the first step in understanding people. If we can't see the innate difference in others and accept them as they are, we will think everyone not like us is at least slightly irregular.

When we understand temperaments, we begin to see why opposites attract. We learn that for a family to have a variety of temperament traits provides a variety of activities and interests. God did not intend us all to be Popular Sanguines. We'd have a lot of fun, but never quite get organized. God did not make us all Powerful Choleric leaders. If He had, there would be none left to follow.

God did not want us all to be Perfect Melancholies, for if things went wrong, we'd all be depressed.

God *did* create Peaceful Phlegmatics as special people to be the buffers for the emotions of the other three, to provide stability and balance.

Peaceful Phlegmatic tones down the wild schemes of Popular Sanguine. Peaceful Phlegmatic refuses to get too impressed with the brilliant decisions of Powerful Choleric. Peaceful Phlegmatic doesn't take too seriously the intricate plans of Perfect Melancholy.

Peaceful Phlegmatic is the great leveler of us all, showing us, "It doesn't really matter that much." And in the long run, it really doesn't! We are all part of a complex plan in which each temperament, when functioning properly, will fit into the right place and unite to form an exciting and balanced picture.

All Purpose

Peaceful Phlegmatic is the easiest of all temperaments to get along with. From the beginning, little Peaceful Phlegmatic babies are blessings to their parents. They will be delightful to have around; they will be happy wherever they're placed; and they will tolerate a flexible schedule. They like friends but are happy alone. Nothing seems to bother them, and they love to watch people pass by.

My son-in-law, Randy, and his father have both shared with me about Randy's Peaceful Phlegmatic childhood. He was easy to get along with and adaptable to any situation. He has always been a serious student, and part of his coin-collecting background came from his constant reading while his parents played bridge many evenings a week. Wherever they went, they took their only child and a few books. Randy would adjust to wherever they placed him, and read without ever causing a fuss. His pleasant disposition and thirst for knowledge have brought him honors as a gold-coin expert and the presidency of the County Numismatic Association. He fits in everywhere and will talk brilliantly or keep quiet, according to the situation. My mother used to say, "That Randy is a saint."

Peaceful Phlegmatic is the closest there is to being a balanced person: one who does not function in the extremes or excesses of life, but walks solidly down the middle road, avoiding conflict and decision on either side. The Peaceful Phlegmatic person does not offend, does not call attention to himself, and quietly does what is expected of him without looking for credit. While Powerful Choleric is the "born leader," Peaceful Phlegmatic is the "learned leader" and with proper motivation can rise to the top because of his outstanding ability to get along with everyone. While Powerful Choleric wants to run everything, Peaceful Phlegmatic tends to hold back until asked and is never pushy.

One day I was in a phone booth at a shopping center, and a young lady recognized my voice from having listened to my *Personality Plus* tapes. As we conversed, Popular Sanguine Burdetta told me she had to call her Peaceful Phlegmatic husband. She was going to ask him to go home to shut off the dryer, so she wouldn't be late for her tennis game. I wasn't sure Fred would have felt this a vital excuse, but she assured me her husband would drop everything to go turn off the dryer with the broken timer so the clothes wouldn't burn up. As she bounced around in her tennis clothes, I asked if she would write up the glories of the perfect Peaceful Phlegmatic husband and here is her response.

Dear Florence,

On Monday, December 14, at a telephone booth in South Coast Plaza, a lady in tennis clothes recognized your voice from your tapes and said hello; that's me! In our conversation you asked for positives about Peaceful Phlegmatics, and I told you I would send you some, since I have been happily married to one for twenty years.

Being Popular Sanguine/Powerful Choleric myself I tend to think only Popular Sanguines are fun to be with and only Powerful Cholerics are worthwhile. Typical Popular Sanguine/Powerful Choleric, I always think my way is the only way.

When I started trying to think of positives for the Peaceful Phlegmatics, the Lord really humbled me. The strength of my life and the stability of my marriage is my Peaceful Phlegmatic husband.

Always calm, slow to anger (Prov. 14:29), in control under stress, never impulsive, logical, reliable, loyal, and patient (Eccles. 7:8). They do not set goals for other people; there are no self-improvement courses for their wives or children, because they sincerely accept people just as they are.

Peaceful Phlegmatics make excellent parents, although they are weak disciplinarians. Their easygoing manner produces contented children.

My ten-year-old son loves baseball and is active in Little League. Win or lose, his father never really cares; he just keeps cheering him on.

They make great bosses. People love to work for them. Because of the lack of pressure or criticism, secretaries seem motivated to give a little extra; their self-esteem is elevated because of this environment and productivity increases.

They make ideal arbitrators. Because of their calm, unemotional logic, they can reduce a tense situation with only a few soft words.

Women Peaceful Phlegmatics have a natural poise that Popular Sanguines admire from far off. They have a quiet ladylike attitude that sets them apart. Their meek and quiet spirit (1 Peter 3:4) is so pleasant to be around.

My Peaceful Phlegmatic husband has a dry sense of humor that comes from not taking life too seriously. When I met you, I was calling his office in Santa Ana to tell him that I had left the dryer on, and ask if he were going up to his Beverly Hills office, could he stop by the house and turn it off. His answer was simply not to worry about it; if the house burns down we'll get another one; then he added a quick little phrase as he hung up—knowing very well that I would never be the one to pay an insurance bill, or even know if we had any—"I'm sure you paid that fire insurance bill that came last week!" His unexpected humor can pull me out of a very serious mood.

Peaceful Phlegmatics really do have redeeming qualities, and I think we should keep them around.

Sincerely,
BURDETTA HONESCKO

Low-Key Personality

Peaceful Phlegmatic is so pleasant and inoffensive to have around that every family should import a few, if they didn't happen to give birth to any. Brenda came to stay with my children for a week, and we all fell in love with her. In the midst of our Powerful Choleric family pressure, Brenda's low-key personality seemed to bring us all into perspective. She agreed with whatever idea was brought up—a trait dearly treasured by Powerful Cholerics, who are always laying plans; and she fit into any slot she was dropped in. No one ever wanted her to leave, and she became part of our family. Six years later she said in Peaceful

Phlegmatic dry humor, "The reason I didn't leave was it was just too much work to pack."

Young Tim became president of his high-school class and was instrumental in leading a protest group to the state capitol. His Popular Sanguine mother was thrilled at his unusually aggressive behavior, and she gathered her friends to watch the six o'clock news when Tim's group would be shown. When the protest march came on, Tim was nowhere in view, until the camera panned the spectators, where his disappointed mother saw him sitting on the curb, with his head in his hands. She was furious, and when he got home she asked why he was not out front leading the group. He replied, "I didn't want to make a fool of myself."

Even if Peaceful Phlegmatic does assume leadership, he will often drop the position before he is seen. He doesn't need the credit, and he surely doesn't want to make a fool of himself.

I asked a young boy about his Peaceful Phlegmatic girlfriend, "What do you like best about her?"

He thought for a minute and said, "I guess all of her, because nothing much stands out." This simple statement sums up Peaceful Phlegmatics; there's nothing that really stands out, but they are such comfortable, well-rounded people to be with. They never appear to be conceited and they keep a low profile. One Peaceful Phlegmatic man said, "I guess I'm just an average person." And another sighed in disbelief, "I'm just amazed when people like me." The humility and gentleness of Peaceful Phlegmatic is so pleasing to be with and gives the other temperaments some positive qualities to work on as we all aim for sainthood.

Easygoing

Peaceful Phlegmatic likes to take it easy and in stages. He doesn't want to think too far ahead. Young Fred had a friend over, and I asked if he'd like to stay for dinner. He replied, "I'll have to think about it. I'll see when the time comes." I set a place for him, and he stayed.

After dinner I put the TV on for him and asked, "Is there anything particular you'd like to watch?"

He said, "Whatever's on."

Later during a commercial, he mumbled, "I did want to see the Dodger game."

I asked, "Why didn't you say so?"

"I was afraid you wouldn't like it." Peaceful Phlegmatic never wants to cause trouble and will quietly accept the status quo rather than ask for a change.

Son Fred has another Peaceful Phlegmatic friend who is so easygoing he hardly moves. One day he was slouched on my couch in torn-up jeans, a ripped T-shirt, scraggly long hair, and bare feet.

I commented, "Mike, it doesn't look as if you spent a lot of time pulling yourself together today."

A Popular Sanguine boy on the other couch spoke up, "Mike believes in the low-maintenance look." What a perfect expression for the Peaceful Phlegmatic.

Calm, Cool, Collected

One of the most admirable traits of Peaceful Phlegmatic is his ability to stay calm in the eye of a storm. Where Popular Sanguine screams, Powerful Choleric lashes out, and Perfect Melancholy sinks down, Peaceful Phlegmatic rides cool. He backs up and waits a minute, and then moves quietly in the right direction. Emotion doesn't overwhelm him; anger doesn't enter his heart. "It's just not worth getting upset over," he muses.

As my brothers and I grew up with a quiet Peaceful Phlegmatic mother, I know we must have caused her many anxious moments. When we would get too wild, she would shut us in the tiny den and say, "I don't care what you do in here, as long as you keep calm, cool, and collected."

Patient—Well Balanced

Peaceful Phlegmatic is never in a hurry, and he doesn't get disturbed over situations that would bother others. Powerful Choleric Gladys told me this story.

> After a day visiting relatives, I could hardly wait to get home. As we got near the freeway, Don said calmly, "We've got to stop for gas." I thought

we could make it, but he didn't want to take the chance, so we drove into a self-service station. I took my little girl to the ladies' room and came out expecting him to be ready to drive away. Instead he was standing by the car holding his money. "Why haven't you paid?" I yelled. "I'm in a hurry." He explained that he didn't know whom to pay.

I spotted a man who looked official and sent him over. Unfortunately, the man wouldn't take the money as he was a customer in his air-force uniform. An attendant appeared and refused the twenty-dollar bill as he could only accept exact change. We didn't have the exact change, and I was mad at the attendant. Don calmly suggested we walk across to a supermarket and get change. I hated to waste the time, but we had no choice. I wanted to barge up to the cashier and ask for change, but Don said that wouldn't be right. We would have to buy something.

"We don't need anything," I countered. He didn't argue, but went to the dairy case where he carefully selected three flavors of yogurt and purchased them with his twenty-dollar bill.

We walked back to the station, and he waited patiently for the attendant to finish changing a tire. When he finally paid his bill, he thanked the man for being understanding, and smiled graciously before joining us in the car. Throughout the whole dreary procedure, he never showed any anger, never got upset with my impatience, and hummed softly all the way home.

Do you see how differently each personality handles situations? Popular Sanguine would not have noticed the gas was low, but if he did, he would have become flustered over how to get the right change. Popular Choleric would have demanded the attendant make the change and caused a scene. Perfect Melancholy would have had the right change, but if not, he would have been disturbed with himself for lack of planning and brooded over it all the way home.

In most situations Peaceful Phlegmatic can be counted on to hold his tongue and to be patient, even under provocation.

Happily Reconciled to Life

Peaceful Phlegmatic doesn't start out with great expectations and is, therefore, more easily reconciled to the vicissitudes of life. He has a basic pessimistic nature that does not depress him as it does Perfect Melancholy, but that keeps him "realistic."

My Peaceful Phlegmatic grandmother used to say to us each night, "I'll see you in the morning, God willing." As a brash teenager I tried to get her to cheer up her good nights, but she made it clear to me, "Some morning I won't get up." And she was right.

When Sue asks her Peaceful Phlegmatic mother how she is today, she replies, "So's to be about," or, "Not so bad as yesterday." Although these are not enthusiastic answers, they keep her from having unreal expectations and then being disappointed.

When I was in college, I asked my mother why she never complimented the three of us. She replied, "If you never say anything too positive, you'll never have to eat your words."

Peaceful Phlegmatic doesn't expect sunshine every day, or a pot of gold at the end of each rainbow, so when rain falls on the Peaceful Phlegmatic's parade he can keep on marching. How much we all could learn from the attitude that accepts life as it is and is reconciled to reality.

Has Administrative Ability

Because Powerful Choleric is noted as the typical business executive, we sometimes overlook Peaceful Phlegmatic as a competent, steady worker—one who gets along with everyone and has administrative ability.

Former President Gerald Ford is Peaceful Phlegmatic, and descriptions of him sound as if they came out of this book.

Bob Pierpoint of CBS said, "Jerry Ford is decent, friendly, compassionate. He didn't really have a new or progressive thought in twenty-five years, but he's a genuinely good guy." Author Doris Goodwin called him "enjoyable, unassuming, relaxed, easygoing, well balanced, normal, decent, honest, regular." The All-American Mr. Clean!

It was Ford's middle-of-the-road, totally inoffensive nature that caused him to be chosen at a moment in history when we didn't want a flashy, daring question mark, but a simple, solid man we could trust. Ford was selected for his Peaceful Phlegmatic personality, even though those choosing probably had no concept of the temperaments.

Long after his defeat for reelection, the *Wall Street Journal* ran an article entitled "Thanks for Nothing."

> We are told the Michigan civic leaders are hesitant to begin raising money for the usual type of commemorative museum for ex-President Gerald R. Ford. One reason, says his old congressional district's Republican chairman, is that the Ford Presidency was "a *passive Presidency rather than an active one*. It was extremely important as a *time of healing*. But how do you make a monument to *something that didn't happen?*"
>
> The chairman has a point there. For a while during those years there was a noticeable letup in the grand domestic schemes, the foreign misadventures and the violent partisanship that had provided most of the drama of American politics for more than a decade. Which may make Gerald Ford a leading candidate for the best and biggest memorial of all.

What a unique honor to be lauded for what you *didn't* do, and praised for what you stayed *out of!* Perfect credits for Peaceful Phlegmatic. One commentator said, "It seemed more important to know who Ford was *not* than to know who he was."

Peaceful Phlegmatic's ability to administer is based on his desire to get along and not rock the boat, as well as his objective overview of people, without having to get involved. School supervisory personnel is heavy with Peaceful Phlegmatics, for they can deal well with both pupil and faculty. Military officials are frequently Peaceful Phlegmatic because they can follow orders, work patiently up through the ranks, not panic under pressure, and not need to be creative or have their own way.

A recent statistic says 80 percent of all people fired from jobs are relieved of their duties because of their inability to get along with people rather than incompetence. Bearing this in mind, it is clear why Peaceful Phlegmatic has an edge over the other temperaments in steady, competent employment.

Mediates Problems

In any area of life there is some kind of conflict: parent/child; teacher/pupil; boss/employee; friend/friend. As the other three temperaments strain and strike, Peaceful Phlegmatic tries to keep peace in the ranks. As men struggle on choppy waters, Peaceful Phlegmatic lifts his head and calms the seas. As others fight for their own way, Peaceful Phlegmatic can sit back and give an objective opinion. Every home and business needs at least one Peaceful Phlegmatic to look at both sides and mete out a calm, cool, and collected reply.

I sat next to a Peaceful Phlegmatic psychologist who told me he was in the ideal profession. "What other temperaments could sit quietly all day, listen to other people's problems, and give an unbiased prescription?"

Warren Christopher, chief U.S. negotiator in the Iran hostage crisis, was praised in a *Los Angeles Times* article by Robert Jackson. Typical Peaceful Phlegmatic terms were: *cool, disciplined, tight-lipped, poker-faced, diplomatic, self-effacing, low-key style, discreet, soft-spoken, collected manner*. He was "the ideal man to deal the cards in the hostage negotiations." He never got angry and he smoothed relations.

The Bible tells us we should be "blameless and harmless, the sons of God, without rebuke . . . " (Phil. 2:15), and Peaceful Phlegmatics come the closest to filling this requirement. They don't cause trouble; they get along with others; and they don't have enemies. Jerry Ford got to the top, not because of brilliant programs, but because he never made enemies on the way up. He once said of himself, "I have lots of adversaries but no enemies I can remember."

Times says of former President George Bush, "He has no fanatical followers, but loads of friends, scarcely a foe, and an impeccable record of public service."

Other temperaments can work hard to win friends and influence people, but this unique ability is the chief gift of Peaceful Phlegmatic. Frequently, I will have a Powerful Choleric man come up to me after a seminar and ask why he was passed up for promotion, after doing all the creative work in the company. Usually the man who got the "big job" was "a dummy" he'd never even noticed, and who had absolutely no credentials. Upon some slight investigation, I usually find "the dummy" was a steady Peaceful Phlegmatic, who did his work well, got along with everyone, and caused no trouble. The Powerful Choleric had dynamic ideas, had forged ahead, and had made many enemies along the way. When it's time to choose the new leader, management frequently reaches for the one who has no enemies.

Easy to Get Along With

Peaceful Phlegmatic has many friends because he is so easy to get along with, and all the other temperaments need such companions. As children and teenagers, Peaceful Phlegmatics are the ones who seldom give a mother trouble and who are joys to have around. Recently Barbara Beuler showed me a copy of a letter she had written to her daughter. It so beautifully expressed the positive qualities of the Peaceful Phlegmatic that I am including it here.

Dear Shara,

As I reflect back on our eighteen years together, I realize how much we have to be thankful for that God blessed us with a Peaceful Phlegmatic daughter. You provide the important balance in the family that includes a Powerful Choleric father, Perfect Melancholy mother, and Popular Sanguine brother. When you were just a baby, you used to play so happily in your playpen with your toys. We had just started our own business in the home, and you fit in so well with the bookkeeping.

Your brother, who is two years older, planned the mischief and the fun. Your famous phrase, which we still tease you about today, was "Me too."

Last Christmas, you were trying desperately to get a word in edgewise, but the whole family was talking noisily and loudly. With your calm, dry sense of humor, you quietly remarked, "Oh, I'll just talk into a tape recorder, and you guys can listen to it later." That got our attention and oh, how we laughed.

I'm so glad, as a mother, that I have been able to have some understanding of the temperaments. When the schoolteacher remarked, "Shara is always late but she is always faithful," I was able to see this with humor.

I remember when a friend confided in you that she wanted to run away from home, you coaxed her to calm down and try to see her parents' point of view.

You so happily accept yourself just as you are, and understand your own temperament so well that you remarked to me, "That's what is so nice about having Peaceful Phlegmatic friends; they hardly ever move, so you always have their phone numbers."

The manager where you work is going to keep you even though business is slow because, in her own words, "Shara is such a good, steady worker and so cheerful with the customers. She works so well with the other employees, and even though it takes her forever to clean the equipment, she cleans it so thoroughly."

Shara, I have enjoyed our very pleasant eighteen years together. I can hardly wait to see how you are going to let your future happen. But I do know, that whatever you decide, you will be committed and content.

Love,

MOM

Has Many Friends

Peaceful Phlegmatic is the greatest friend of all, because his total assets add up to positive human relations. He is easygoing, relaxed, calm, cool, well balanced, patient, consistent, peaceful, inoffensive, and pleasant. What more could anyone ever ask in a friend? The Peaceful Phlegmatic friend always has time for you. When you visit a Powerful Choleric girlfriend, she is polishing, rearranging, or folding, while you both are conversing, giving you the feeling that her time is too valuable to spend on you alone. The Peaceful Phlegmatic friend will drop everything, sit down, and relax.

I had one Peaceful Phlegmatic friend who was a great mother to her brood, but housework was not a high priority. If I dropped by in the middle of the morning, the kitchen table would still have the cereal bowls, the open boxes, and the milk from breakfast. We'd both sit down, push the debris to one side, make room for our elbows, and enjoy each other's company. Since the mess didn't bother her, it didn't bother me.

Is a Good Listener

Another reason Peaceful Phlegmatics have many friends is that they are good listeners. As a group, Peaceful Phlegmatics would rather listen than talk. Peaceful Phlegmatic can keep quiet. He doesn't have to say a word, and other temperaments love to have people they can spout off to in time of need. Popular Sanguines, especially, need Peaceful Phlegmatic friends who will let them talk and provide a responsive audience. When I was the president of the Women's Club of San Bernardino, I had a perfect Peaceful Phlegmatic friend, Lucy, next door. Each Wednesday after the meeting I would stop at her home and tell her all the frustrating and hilarious stories about my club day. She would listen, smile, commiserate, and nod, and when I'd said it all, she'd thank me for coming and I would leave.

All Popular Sanguines need good, quiet Peaceful Phlegmatic friends!

Gentle words cause life and health; griping brings discouragement.

Proverbs 15:4 TLB

PART THREE

Personality Plan

A Way to Overcome Our Personal Weaknesses

Positives Carried to Extremes Become Negatives

In each one of us are good and bad—we have traits that are positive and traits that produce negative responses in others. Quite often the same characteristics can be both a plus and a minus, according to degree, and many positives carried to extremes become negatives.

Popular Sanguine's great ability to carry on a colorful conversation whether in the Co-op or the Congo is a plus envied by others; *but* carried to extremes Popular Sanguine is constantly talking, monopolizing, interrupting, and straying too far from the truth.

Perfect Melancholy's deep analytical thinking is a genius trait, much respected by those of lighter minds; *yet* carried to extremes, he becomes brooding and depressed.

Powerful Choleric's gift for quick, incisive leadership is desperately needed in every phase of life today; *but* carried to extremes, Powerful Choleric becomes bossy, controlling, and manipulative.

Peaceful Phlegmatics easygoing nature is an admirable combination that makes him the favorite of any group; *yet* carried to extremes, Peaceful Phlegmatic doesn't care about doing anything and is indifferent and indecisive.

As we look at each one of these temperaments with an eye to examining ourselves, we should note those attributes that cause positive responses in others and lift our self-image. Then we should reflect on these characteristics. Then we should pay special attention to those extremes of behavior that are offensive to others, and, finally, pledge to ourselves that we will dedicate our human and spiritual resources to overcoming these problem areas.

Remember all the great heroes we studied in Shakespeare: Hamlet, Macbeth, King Lear, and the Henrys? They all were great men who accomplished much, but each one had a "tragic flaw" that caused his downfall.

Each one of us has hero blood within our veins, and how exciting it is to discover our strengths and use them wisely! But as with these men of old, each one of us has some "tragic flaw," which, left untended, may result in a downfall for us. Let's each one of us examine ourselves realistically and find our flaws before it is too late.

> *If you refuse criticism you will end in poverty and disgrace; if you accept criticism you are on the road to fame.*
>
> Proverbs 13:18 TLB

CHAPTER 8

Let's Organize Popular Sanguine

Popular Sanguines are the most willing of all to change, because they love new ideas and projects, and because they are sincerely devoted to being popular and inoffensive. There are two major problems, however, that keep Popular Sanguines from making the necessary improvements.

No Follow-Through

First, while they have good intentions, they seldom follow through on any given plan. After I explain to a Popular Sanguine what he has to do to overcome his weaknesses, I ask, "When are you going to put this into action?" Usually the person will say, "I can't start today, and I'll be out of town tomorrow—and we've got company for the weekend." Right there they've lost the fight.

No-Fault People

Second, they are such a fun-loving group, with such engaging personalities, they can't really believe they have any major faults. They don't really take themselves seriously.

When I go over Popular Sanguine weaknesses in a seminar, they all laugh at them but don't feel they're bad enough to demand action. I understand, because I felt the same way. Before I was married, I was adorable and the life of the party, but overnight I became stupid. Fred let me know that I might have been cute in Haverhill, but I wasn't very funny in New York. It never occurred to me he was right; I figured he was dull and unappreciative. So I played the role he wanted from me when I was with him, and was my own charming self with others. It wasn't until I began studying the personalities that my eyes were opened to the fact that Fred was not alone in his opinions.

As I became aware that my weaknesses weren't all in Fred's head, I developed some suggestions for me and other Popular Sanguines.

PROBLEM: *Popular Sanguines Talk Too Much*
Solution 1: **Talk Half as Much as Before**

Since Popular Sanguines have no feel for figures, it would be wasted advice to suggest cutting conversation by 22 percent, but they do have a general grasp of half of anything. Good guidelines would be for you Popular Sanguines to talk half as much as before. The simple way to control yourself is to delete every other story you are compelled to tell. You will feel sorry for what the public is missing, but they will never know what they didn't hear, and that's all to the good. It's better to have the group enjoy what you said than be stifled by your total control of the conversation—no matter how adorable your stories may be.

Can You Top This?

Fred and I went to the family reunion caused by the death of his ninety-seven-year-old grandmother. On the first day together, the gathering resembled a "Can You Top This" television program. Each relative felt led to chronicle the glories of his career, only to be overwhelmed by the next brother. That night in our room Fred came up with what proved to be a terrible idea: "Why don't we keep quiet and see how long it is before anyone asks us a question or pulls us into the conversation?" I didn't like this plan right from the start, but I figured I could wait out a few hours.

We started our repressive routine right after breakfast, continued through lunch, all afternoon, through dinner and the evening. By the time we got to our room, my eyes were bulging out of my head with pressure, and I thought I was going to explode. "This is ridiculous!" I cried. "I can't stand this another minute."

Fred smiled, "I've enjoyed every minute of it, and we'll try it again tomorrow."

"Another day of suppressed stories? I'll have a nervous breakdown!"

We did have another full day of suppressed stories, and I did not have a nervous breakdown. It was close—but I survived.

The next morning, before we left for the plane, Fred's mother said, "You've been quiet for the last hour, Fred. Is there something wrong?" He assured her he was fine, and she patted him and said, "Lovely, dearie, lovely."

The worst insult was that neither she nor anyone else ever noticed I had said nothing for two full days. Here I had a lifetime record and didn't even get a trophy! But I did learn a painful lesson: The world can get along—even seem relatively happy—if I don't open my mouth. Therefore, my new role of talking only half as much as before seems like a reprieve.

Why don't you Popular Sanguines see how long you can go mute before someone notices the change?

Solution 2: Watch for Signs of Boredom

The other three temperaments wouldn't need to be told what "signs of boredom" are, but the Popular Sanguines, unable to even entertain the thought they might be boring, need to be clearly told that when a person is pulling away from your grip, that means they've lost interest in your tale. When your audience stands on tiptoe, glancing desperately over the crowd, trying to catch someone's eye, they want *out*. When they break away to go to the bathroom and never return, you should get the hint. The signs aren't difficult to notice, once you entertain the possibility.

Solution 3: Condense Your Comments

"Get to the point," is a statement Fred has made to me for about forty years, perhaps because I've never felt the point was really the point. I've adhered to the slogan "telling them is half the fun." Consequently, I've rarely made a simple statement. I tend to overdress the drama. Likewise, I would be embarrassed to expose a naked story stripped to the bare bones.

While I've always felt this gift for storytelling was an asset, carried to extremes it becomes a liability. I have learned that not everyone has the time or interest to last out a Popular Sanguine monologue. Although I feel the total historical background is essential for understanding a current comment, I have found no one seems to suffer if spared one detail (or even a dozen).

One day I came up with a provocative idea. I made an agreement with myself that if I was in the middle of a perfectly charming story, and it was somehow interrupted, I would not pick the thread up again until someone asked me to continue. My first test came as a group of us was heading on a shopping trip. I was in the middle of a delightful story when, at a critical point with the heroine at the edge of a cliff, the driver asked to see the map to make sure she was heading in the right direction. I held my breath, waiting for someone to ask, "And then what happened?" but no one did. I stayed on the edge of my seat, ready to spring into verbal action, but no one ever looked my way. Didn't they care what happened to Harriet? I wanted to shake them and say, "Remember Harriet? She was hanging over a cliff. Don't you want to hear the rest?" I remembered my pledge to myself: *Don't finish unless asked*; and no one asked.

This rejection was an unbelievable answer to my test. People sometimes do get so weary of a long, amplified story that they just don't care how the whole thing turns out—even when I'm the one telling it.

My Popular Sanguine friend Nancy agreed to test out the same theory and got the same results. We've made a quiet pact between us that when this trauma falls upon either one of us, the other will eagerly say, "Go on, go on! I can hardly wait to hear the rest!" Oh, how I love Nancy!

Solution 4: Stop Exaggerating

When I began to give my testimony in public, my husband said, "Now that you're a Christian speaker, don't you think it's time you stopped lying?" I knew I didn't lie, and I asked him what he meant. As a Perfect Melancholy, he felt when I didn't tell the exact truth, I was lying. I felt I was just being colorful, so we settled on the term *exag-*

gerating. Later I heard Lauren tell a young friend, "When you listen to my mother you have to cut everything in half."

One day I went to Popular Sanguine Patti's new home, and when I walked in she greeted me with "Every dog and cat on this street is dying of mange." My Popular Sanguine mind instantly pictured dozens of dying dogs and cats, gasping their last breaths in the gutter. As I was captured by this mental scene, I noticed her Perfect Melancholy daughter shaking her head in despair.

"What's the matter?" I asked her, and she replied, "The lady next door has a sick cat."

No one could get too excited over some unknown woman's sick cat, but "Every dog and cat on the street is dying of mange" is really an opener!

Fred and I were once at a party where a delightful Popular Sanguine girl named Bonnie enthralled the group with her detailed description of a boat trip from Los Angeles to Catalina Island. She relived the entertainment for us all, recited the menu, told who got seasick, and held our attention for twenty minutes. As soon as she concluded her hilarious story about their boat trip to Catalina, her Perfect Melancholy husband took a deep breath and said, quietly but firmly, two words: *We flew*.

We all stood stunned as Bonnie reflected for a moment and then agreed, "That's right, we flew."

Only a Popular Sanguine could spend twenty minutes describing in detail a trip she'd never taken on a boat she'd never boarded.

Although Popular Sanguines' stories are funny and I'll never forget this incident, Bonnie had gone so far in her exaggerations that she was lying. A friend told me a similar situation this morning and concluded with "Of course she's a Popular Sanguine, so you can't believe a word she says." Isn't that a shame? Isn't it too bad Popular Sanguines can't be trusted to deal anywhere near the truth? Think it over and check yourself.

REMEMBER

Colorful carried to extremes becomes lying.

PROBLEM: *Popular Sanguines Are Self-Centered*
Solution 1: Be Sensitive to Other People's Interests

Popular Sanguines are the least sensitive to others because they are so wrapped up in themselves. They are so happy with their own stories, they don't notice the attention span of others and may talk way beyond the interest of the group. They seldom notice the needs of others because they innately avoid problems or negative situations. Popular Sanguines don't make good counselors because they'd rather talk than listen, and they tend to give quick simplistic answers that may not be appropriate.

Learning to be sensitive to others starts with *listening* and *looking*. I have trained myself to enter groups quietly and listen until I get the grasp of the conversation rather than blurting right out my newest story. Many times I've been grateful I hesitated first, *before* putting my foot in my open mouth. I have worked at looking at people as individuals and not just as audience material.

As I have tuned in to others, I have discovered so many hurting people I'd overlooked before; so many lonely ladies that Popular Sanguines tend to avoid; so many broken hearts that need mending; so many heavy-laden bodies that need the light touch of a Popular Sanguine.

From here on, Popular Sanguines, listen to and look at each person as someone special, and you will become sensitive to others' needs.

Solution 2: Learn to Listen

The reason Popular Sanguines don't listen is not that they have a genetic problem, but because they care only about themselves. Listening is a gracious gesture, and Popular Sanguines aren't concerned enough to force themselves to become interested in others. They feel life is a theater, where they are on stage, and everyone else is in the audience. The very best of Popular Sanguines can get away with the entertainer image, but most of us come across as egotists when we keep everyone's eyes focused on us.

REMEMBER

Be sensitive to others' needs
and listen to what they have to say.

PROBLEM: *Popular Sanguines Have Uncultivated Memories*

Solution 1: Pay Attention to Names

The reason Popular Sanguines don't remember names is as I stated earlier: They don't listen, and they don't care. Both of these problems stem from their self-centered natures and their insensitivity to others. They may be fun to be with but people sense they don't care when they can't remember minutes later who the others are.

Dale Carnegie said, "The sweetest sound in the world is a person's name." In his *How to Win Friends* book he gives many examples of people whose success was related to how well they concentrated on learning the names of others.

Popular Sanguines aren't any less intelligent than other temperaments, and they can remember names once they decide it's important. Powerful Cholerics know how crucial it is to call people by name. Perfect Melancholies have good minds for holding on to detail, and Peaceful Phlegmatics love to watch and listen, but Popular Sanguines are deficient in all these areas. They don't think anything is crucial enough to work at; they aren't tuned in to details; and they would much rather talk than listen. Is there any hope?

For all of my married life I have found it was easier to ask Fred people's names than learn them myself—and it was. When I first studied temperaments, I realized this dependence on Fred's mind showed I couldn't depend on mine. I asked myself, "Are you so stupid you have to hire a brain? Can't you learn yourself?" That question made me realize I'd never seriously tried to remember names, and I decided to get to work on a new hobby. Popular Sanguines have to make it a game. *First,* I began to listen to people's names, a step so simple anyone can do it, and without which there is little hope for improvement. We can hardly hold on to what we never hear. As I forced my mind to concentrate as people spoke, I learned everyone has a name and likes to be called by it.

How amazed and impressed I am when someone can handle *Littauer* instead of making it Littenouer, Littoner, Littaver, Littenhauser, or Latouer. How happy others will be with me if I can handle their handle. There's a great motivation for a Popular Sanguine: *Others will like us better*. Isn't that what we really want? A key to popularity is knowing who others are.

Second, I began to care about others. I began to look at them when they said their names, and question them about their lives, until I felt I knew them. How much more interesting people have become since I've learned to take my eyes off myself and turn them toward others.

Solution 2: **Write Things Down**

While the Popular Sanguine memory for color and trivia is even beyond the facts, their memory for names, dates, and places is almost nonexistent. This division of the mind is understandable, when we realize the Popular Sanguine temperament is far more interested in people than in statistics, and in colorful fiction than cold facts. Perfect Melancholy loves details and remembers the essentials of life, so if we looked on the positives, we would always team the two together: Perfect Melancholy to get it right and Popular Sanguine to make it interesting.

Fred has a fantastic ability to remember names, helped by his plan of writing everyone's name down on a little card, with some pertinent fact about them. When we lived in Connecticut, we had a Popular Sanguine pastor who couldn't remember one parishioner from another. Fred helped him out by standing next to him at the door on Sunday morning and giving him instant biographies under his breath as each unfamiliar person approached.

"This lady in the pink dress is Walda Worry. She has six children and her husband's in the hospital with back trouble."

"Walda, dear, you look lovely in pink! How are those adorable little children? And how's your poor husband's back coming along?"

Fred fed the facts; Don did the decorating.

After we left Connecticut, Don's memory had an instant retreat, and people wondered why his charming concern had turned into a desperate grasping for names. One day he asked a lady how her husband was feeling when, in fact, he had just conducted the poor man's funeral two days before.

We have a Popular Sanguine friend Tommy who ironically teaches a memory course. He does an exciting job at communicating the principles, and people do learn, but it hasn't helped *him* in everyday life. One day I stopped by and found him searching wildly through his garage. He had lost two cases of memory books he needed for a course that night, and he couldn't remember where he'd put them.

Since Popular Sanguines have such poor memories, they must write down lists of what they have to do, and keep the lists where they won't lose them. They must take notes on people's names and review them before going to the same group again. They must make sure, before they make business calls, that they have all their facts before them. A good mind can appear stupid when it's groping for information it should know.

Solution 3: **Don't Forget the Children**

I've met many Popular Sanguine women who had lost at least a child or two at some time in their motherhood. One drove an hour into the desert, chatting happily with her Popular Sanguine friend, before noticing her four-year-old was not in the back seat. She drove back to the gas station where she'd started, and there was her little boy helping the man pump gas. The attendant was grateful she'd returned because he was about to go home, and didn't know what to do with his new assistant.

One lady told me she had forgotten to pick up her child from the third grade and didn't realize it until the family sat down for dinner and his seat was empty.

In a Popular Sanguine group report from one of our seminars the chairman stated, "We took a survey and among us we had lost four hundred and thirty-seven things this week, including seven children and one grandmother, tragically abandoned in a department store."

My Popular Sanguine friend Carol and I carpooled when our two Perfect Melancholy sons were in their early grades. We were both frequently late, and while we understood each other, the boys were constantly depressed. When I would go to pick up James, Jr., he would come out mournfully, carrying a bowl of cereal.

"My mother was on the phone again, and I had to take care of myself."

Fred, Jr., would arrive home whenever Carol happened to get him there, and he would always have tales of how she forgot him, or how she almost drove into the back of a truck. Carol and I met recently in Dallas and laughed over our forgetful years of carpooling. We decided our inconsistency was good for the boys because it taught them flexibility.

Popular Sanguines have the creative ability to take their obvious weaknesses and find ways to turn them into strengths.

REMEMBER

Even though you can rationalize why you have a bad memory, no one wants to hear about it. Pay attention to people's names, write things down, and try to take note of where you left your car and your child.

PROBLEM: *Popular Sanguines Are Fickle and Forgetful Friends*

Solution 1: Read *The Friendship Factor*

While Popular Sanguines have many friends because they keep life exciting, they are not usually "good friends." They're happy to be around, but they fade off into the wings when there are needs or troubles. They might be called "fair-weather friends." I had one Popular Sanguine buddy who was a "wet-weather friend." She only called me when it was pouring rain and she couldn't play golf.

Popular Sanguines tend to have fans or groupies more than real friends. They collect people who admire them, love them, and (hopefully) worship them. They like those who are giving but look the other way when needs arise. They are too busy with the excitement and glamour to take time for the troubles.

When I read *The Friendship Factor* by Alan L. McGinnis (Augsburg Press), I realized for the first time I had not been much of a friend, although I had many acquaintances. Dr. McGinnis challenged me to examine my life in the areas of lasting relationships, and I saw that I was letting some dear friends drift away because it wasn't easy to get together.

In 1980 I invited forty women from all over the country to come to Redlands, California, for a Speakers' Training Seminar. Thirty-six came, and in one week together we became friends. We shared our hearts with each other and didn't want to separate. To keep these friendships going, I sent out a letter reviewing what each had written me and keeping them posted on each other. I also started a Wednesday-morning group at my home for the women in my area. We all agreed we would have drifted apart if we hadn't disciplined ourselves to come together in fellowship once a week.

Solution 2: **Put Others' Needs First**

Popular Sanguines rarely make the effort to be true friends, to care for the needy, and visit the sick. When I was president of the Women's Club of San Bernardino, it was expected I should go to the hospital when members were ill. This was so foreign to my nature that I found it difficult to do. I would find excuses, and once I arrived to visit one member's husband, only to find he'd died the day before. I had to convince myself that others' needs were important and then discipline myself to act accordingly. Many times when I had to force myself to go somewhere, the Lord blessed me with a rich experience.

REMEMBER

Popular Sanguines, it's not easy to be a "good friend"
but it's more than worth the effort. Don't settle for
an audience; become a friend.

PROBLEM: *Popular Sanguines Interrupt and Answer for Others.*

Solution: Don't Think You Must Fill All the Gaps

I used to feel God had appointed me the Official Gap Filler of Life. Since I always had something to say and I couldn't stand silence, I would jump in with a story as soon as someone drew a quick breath. I never felt I was interrupting, but rather that I was saving the audience from a dull experience. I took on the role of the little Dutch boy with his finger in the dike, keeping the whole city from being washed away with water. I looked at conversation as a big protective wall that could not afford holes, and as one emerged, I would dash to fill the void lest the group be engulfed by boredom.

Fred found this frenzied gap-filling Florence to be too effusive, and he tried to tell me Silence Is Golden, and there is nothing wrong with calm dead air once in a while. I ignored his request for serenity until I understood my temperament and realized that Popular Sanguines do have this compulsion for plugging all conversation holes. As I began to bite my tongue and forcibly keep my lips from moving, I noticed Fred began to talk. Attention shifted from me to him, and I found he had something intelligent to say.

One engaging Popular Sanguine girl, Sharon, told me how she had been sick at the time of her church Christmas party and had been unable to go. Later friends mentioned to Sharon how charming her husband had been at the party, and how they had never known he had much personality. She thought this over and realized she had never given him much of a chance to shine. From then on she worked at leaving a few gaps open for him to fill and was amazed to see he was able to do it.

Non-Phlegmatic Phil

One day I flipped on the TV and caught "The Phil Donahue Show." Phil was interviewing Economist Adam Smith, and I was amazed at the perfect temperament study they both were: Phil, the extrovert Popular Sanguine/Powerful Choleric, focusing all attention on himself; Adam, deep Perfect Melancholy (with a genius mind) and Peaceful Phlegmatic (very low key, witty) and unruffled by questions.

Phil's comments showed a lack of knowledge of temperaments and an assumption that because Adam's personality was not volatile like his, he was a little dull.

> PHIL: I can see you are not too excited about this subject.
> ADAM: I'm very excited. I just don't have your energy.
> PHIL: I can tell you're bored.
> ADAM: I'm not bored. This is just the face I was born with.

When the audience asked questions of Adam, Phil jumped in with the answers. At one point, Phil turned to Adam, after giving a full response for him, and said, "That is how you feel about this, isn't it, Adam?" And Adam replied, "Why ask me?"

There was no need to ask him, for Phil was having a great time telling everyone what he assumed Adam would say. Popular Sanguine always feels he should answer for everyone else, because he can say it so much better.

In our home both Marita and I give quick answers to everyone's questions. One evening at dinner, Fred asked Freddie how things went at school. Marita immediately answered, "He had to sit outside by the principal's office, so he must have been bad."

She didn't even go to the same school, but she had driven by and spotted him seated at the office door. Freddie was not pleased with her report and Father Fred instituted a new rule that Marita and I have never liked: *Only the one being asked the question is allowed to respond.*

This discipline slows down the conversation and sometimes results in utter silence, while one quiet member musters up his thoughts for a simple presentation.

As you become more familiar with the temperaments you will notice how quickly Popular Sanguines answer for others, and how they do not even notice they are doing it.

REMEMBER

One who interrupts and answers for others is rude
and inconsiderate, and after a while, unwelcome.

PROBLEM: *Popular Sanguine Is Disorganized and Immature*

Solution 1: Pull Your Life Together

While Popular Sanguines are often the ones voted "Most Likely to Succeed," they frequently don't succeed. They have the ideas, the personality, the creativity, but they seldom get it all pulled together at any given time. If they happen to hit instant success, they ride high, but if it takes years of planning and work, they will quit and head off in another direction. Many Popular Sanguines change jobs, even careers, every few years because they see the crown is elusive in this kingdom, so they'd better move on.

Many Popular Sanguines become pastors because they like the platform ministry, and love to have "all eyes on me" for at least an hour a week. Although they are charming and entertaining, they are frequently ill-prepared and often trying to pull themselves together at the last minute.

One wedding I attended was conducted by a handsome pastor. He came out before the wedding, clipped on his mike, and announced the opening song. Suddenly a look of panic came over his face; he took off his mike, and he ran back and forth between the two pulpits searching through papers. He had forgotten the book where he had written the couple's names, and he had no idea who they were. The wedding march started, so he ran back to position, clipped on the mike, and gave a big smile to the audience. The service was charming and personal but with unusual vows with no names mentioned. Suddenly he got a bright idea. He stopped and asked the couple to kneel for one minute of silent prayer. He instructed the congregation and the wedding party to bow their heads, close their eyes, and meditate. While they were doing as he asked, he quickly took off the mike, bolted out the side door, ran across the patio, and disappeared into his office. Instantly he emerged carrying a book, tiptoed back in place, clipped on his mike, took a deep breath, and said, "Amen." He then opened the book and proceeded to read the rest of the ceremony correctly. (The silent prayer kept most heads down, but naturally I peeked, and Fred clocked the trip at forty-seven seconds.)

While Popular Sanguine stories are funny, they show that the Popular Sanguine means well but seldom reaches his potential. He doesn't want to get down to work today. Something always comes up. Pleasure outranks work.

In counseling experiences, I find the Popular Sanguine most willing to agree that he must get down to work and get organized. He will admit he has not achieved what he set out to do in life, and he wants to improve. I spend time showing him what to do and send him out to do it. He means well, but things come up and he can't quite get to it. By the time he remembers he was going to make some changes, he's lost the list, and it probably wouldn't have worked anyway.

Does this sound like any of you? You Popular Sanguines have the greatest potential of all. It is possible for a Popular Sanguine to reach the top of anything, but you must start today to pull your life together. If you wait until tomorrow something will come up.

Solution 2: Grow Up

> Ye Younglings!
> Ye Popular Sanguine, shallow hearted boys

Shakespeare knew temperaments, and in writing about Popular Sanguines, referred to one of their greatest weaknesses—their desire to never grow up. Popular Sanguines live like Peter Pan and want to fly off to Never-Never Land rather than face the harsh realities of life.

No business or marriage can function profitably when one, or both, of the partners refuses to grow up. Maturity does not depend on age; it depends on our willingness to face our responsibilities and make realistic plans to meet them.

David cried out, "Oh that I had wings like a dove! for then would I fly away . . . " (Ps. 55:6). But he didn't run away from trouble, he faced it squarely, called upon God for help in time of trouble, and overcame what seemed like insurmountable odds.

REMEMBER

The Popular Sanguine needs a Savior.
Without divine help how can he:
Curb his tongue.
Control his ego.
Not think too highly of himself.
Cultivate his memory.
(The Holy Spirit gives remembrance.)
Concern himself with others.
Look out for others and not for himself.
Count the cost.

I can do all things through Christ which strengtheneth me.

Philippians 4:13

CHAPTER **9**

Let's Cheer Up
Perfect Melancholy

The Perfect Melancholy person is a study in contrasts. He has the highest highs and the lowest lows. He loves the study of the temperaments because it gives him analytical tools to use in his constant search for introspection—and yet he resists the temperaments because he is afraid the theory is too simple, too easy to understand, and is not deep enough to be significant. He refuses to be put in a box with a label, because he feels that, unlike other temperaments, he is a unique being, complex, not known even to himself, and surely not able to be put in any general grouping.

One of a Kind?

The one amazing constant in the true Perfect Melancholy is his belief that no one else in life is just like him. He has always been able to prove to himself that he is right and the world is wrong. He knows he could be happy if others would be like him.

One of the most amazing benefits we have found in our seminars is in showing the Perfect Melancholies they are not unusual. Others do think, look, and act as they do. When we divide the audience into groups, according to how they score on their Personality Profile, the Perfect Melancholies file out reluctantly. They don't want to "play games," and heaven forbid they should relax and have fun! When they do get together, however, it is as if the veil has been lifted. They all pull their chairs up neatly to the table; they all are dressed meticulously; they all have their pens in hand; and they all are suspicious of one another.

As they look around and begin to analyze the group, the light goes on, and they see they *are* similar. As they all quietly inspect each other, they see there is validity to the study of the temperaments. Sometimes a smile or two is seen as they recognize the unity evident in the group.

One man told me this moment of truth was the changing point in his marriage. He had come to our seminar at the insistence of his Popular Sanguine wife, who had left him twice before and was about to again. In his eyes, all their problems were because of her. She took life too lightly; she had won all the children to her side by what must be bribery; and she had failed to master housework in twenty-eight years of marriage. He lived alone in a house with eight children by shutting himself away physically, mentally, and emotionally—leaving her to cope.

As he went off to the Perfect Melancholy group that day in Phoenix, he did so with no desire to learn a thing; he told me he was shocked to sit and look around the table and see clones of himself.

"At that very instant," he said, "I could see what my wife had been looking at all these years. I could see in the faces of the others the reflection of me. I could see the depth and seriousness of purpose, but I could also see a superior attitude and a total lack of humor. I went home that night and apologized to my wife for being her stone-faced judge for twenty-eight years. She cried and said, 'I never thought you'd be able to see yourself as others see you. Thank God.'

"As I put my arms around her with a warmth and acceptance I'd not ever shown, I knew our marriage had been healed."

How much we can learn if we examine those traits that apply to our basic temperament and learn from them!

PROBLEM: *Perfect Melancholies Are Easily Depressed*

Solution 1: **Realize No One Likes Gloomy People**

A cartoon by Colman titled "Men and Women" shows a couple facing each other. He looks depressed and she says, "If this is *happy*, what are you like when you're *sad*?" With Perfect Melancholies it is sometimes hard to tell happy from sad, because they don't ever want to get too excited, and most of life is serious—if not downright depressing. While Perfect Melancholy is offended by the loud, manipulative Powerful Choleric, what he doesn't realize is how he controls others by his moods. As people learn what turns him off, they try their best to not trigger him into a decline. This touchy relationship is difficult at best, and people try to avoid contact, if possible.

Once you Perfect Melancholies realize what you are doing with your moods, you can begin to improve. As Popular Sanguine has to force himself to get organized, you have to force yourself to be cheerful. As I explained this principle to my son, he countered, "But I don't *feel* cheerful."

"You don't have to *feel* cheerful, just *be* cheerful. I'd rather have phony *joy* than genuine depression."

Realize no one likes gloomy people. Even if you have every reason in the world to go hang yourself, no one wants to hear about it. As Perfect Melancholies get older, they tend to get more mournful. They decide no one loves them anymore, and then set out to prove themselves right. The little widow sits there feeling lonely. A nice lady from the church comes by and asks, "How are you today?"

The Perfect Melancholy, taking life seriously, tells her every problem she's had in a month. She goes on and on in dreary detail, ending with—"And no one ever comes to see me."

The nice visitor drags herself out into the sunlight and determines never to go see her again. Her name is then added to the mental list of those who don't come anymore, and the Perfect Melancholy has perpetuated her own negative beliefs. If only Perfect Melancholies could realize that no one likes gloomy people, they could work toward a less pessimistic view of life.

Solution 2: Don't Look for Trouble

Perfect Melancholies tend to take everything too personally, and they frequently look for trouble. One girl told me, "My husband is so negative, if we go to see a bad movie, he makes me feel like I produced it."

Perfect Melancholies have particularly hard times with Popular Sanguine/Powerful Cholerics because they *blurt* out whatever goes through their minds without thinking of the consequences. Because Perfect Melancholy has preplanned each statement, he assumes others have also, and therefore, he reads into each casual comment a deep, hidden meaning.

As you Perfect Melancholies begin to understand the different temperaments, a big weight will be lifted from you. You will realize, perhaps for the first time, that the Popular Sanguine/Powerful Cholerics are not out to get you. They haven't given you that much thought, and they surely have not planned ahead. As you learn to evaluate others by their set of temperament traits (and not by your own), you will have a whole new outlook on people. You can smile at each passing person, and stop looking for trouble.

Perfect Melancholies often feel left out and wonder why they are not invited to social events; and yet, when approached, they frequently turn people off with their negative responses. One day we asked such a woman to come to a party at our home. Instead of showing any enthusiasm, she replied, "Well, I'll be out all day and won't accomplish a thing, so I guess I might as well blow the whole night too."

Sometimes a Perfect Melancholy can take a positive situation and turn it into a negative. The last time I went to the hairdresser, he sighed as soon as I sat down, and said, "Your daughter is sure giving me trouble." I assumed Marita must have been late for an appointment, and I asked, "What has she done wrong?" He replied, "She keeps sending me new customers. She's sent me at least ten new ones this month, and what's worse, they like me and keep coming back!"

A friend gave me this list she found on her grandmother's dresser:

JEAN HASN'T SENT ME A CHRISTMAS CARD IN TWO YEARS
SUE DIDN'T KISS ME GOOD-BYE
EVELYN CAME OUT INTO HER YARD AND DIDN'T SAY HI
RUTH DIDN'T RUN ME AROUND TODAY AS I ASKED
HAZEL WON'T COME TO VISIT GRANDPA AND SAYS HE'S NOT HER RESPONSI-
    BILITY

Who knows how the grandmother was planning to use this information, but she was writing it down so she'd never forget.

To test the theory that Perfect Melancholies really remember the negatives, I asked a group of musicians I was working with if they could recall any incident in which a teacher in their first few grades had done them in. Instantly all hands went up, and we listened for thirty minutes as they gave the details of their demises.

One told of the kindergarten teacher who wouldn't let him have milk with his graham crackers; one of how he was accused of pulling the pigtail of the girl in front of him, when it was really the boy in the green shirt; and one was still hurt over the teacher who pinned a note on him, showing she didn't think he was smart enough to carry it home.

Fred can recall many incidents of his childhood in which he felt put upon. He was the middle child of five and thought he was not old enough to get the privileges and too old to get the attention. In the family movies he's frequently in tears, and his brothers called him "Wha Wha" for Crybaby. Although he now knows his problems were accentuated by his Perfect Melancholy temperament, he can still recall negative incidents vividly.

My Perfect Melancholy son, Fred, gets close to excited when a wing of the school burns down, or when there was a drug raid and half the eighth grade was sent to jail. Nothing short of tragedy moves him, and he enjoys focusing on the negatives.

It is only logical to assume that when one spends much mental energy dwelling on negatives, such a mind falls easily into depression. Perfect Melancholy needs to keep his thoughts on the positives, and the minute he finds himself focusing on the negative aspect of *anything*, he must refuse those thoughts an entrance. "Thou wilt keep him in perfect peace, whose mind is stayed on thee . . . " (Isa. 26:3). " . . . If there be any virtue, and if there be any praise, think on these things" (Phil. 4:8).

Solution 3: Don't Get Hurt So Easily

Perfect Melancholies actually enjoy getting hurt and this problem again focuses their eyes on themselves and how "put upon" they are. When my husband, Fred, was a teenager, he was deeply Perfect Melancholy, and he noticed he was not getting his share of the outside cuts of the Sunday roast. Since everyone in the family liked the spicy edges, and Fred felt he was neglected, he began to keep a "Roast Beef Chart."

For sixteen weeks he wrote his entries each Sunday: *Jan. 12*, AUNT EDIE AND DICK; *Jan. 19*, STEVE AND GRANDPA. . . . One day his mother was cleaning his room, and she lifted the blotter on his desk. Here was this strange list with all these dates and names. When he came home, she asked him what it was, and he smugly told her, "This is the chart of who got the outside cuts of the roast beef. You will notice that in sixteen weeks my name does not appear. Now I have proof of how neglected I am."

His Powerful Choleric mother could hardly believe he would take the time to keep a record of the end cuts of the Sunday roast, but he reveled in negative truth.

Many Perfect Melancholies go out of their way to be hurt. Right from the beginning little Perfect Melancholies feel left out or neglected. Here's an example:

> On Christmas, six-year-old Joshua had a predictably unsatisfactory day. First of all, he took inventory of his "toy" presents and those of his cousin Laura. He found she had received more. Although Joshua had new clothes and Star Wars bedding, he had tears streaming down his face as he cried, "Santa Claus likes Laura better!"

Solution 4: **Look for the Positives**

Perfect Melancholies gather criticism that no one ever made. If they hear their name mentioned across the room, they will *know* people are saying bad things about them. In contrast, Popular Sanguines feel that if they're being talked about at all, it's good. They believe the old adage, "There's no such thing as bad publicity."

The Perfect Melancholy mind is like a radio dial on which the station is set on *negative*, but much of the emphasis can be changed when Perfect Melancholy decides to look for the silver lining, instead of sitting under the black cloud. Look for the best in people, and when things go wrong, thank God for the experience and ask Him what positive lesson you are to learn from this. " . . . Happy [is] the man who puts his trust in the Lord" (Prov. 16:20 TLB).

Solution 5: Read *Blow Away the Black Clouds*

In my book *Blow Away the Black Clouds* (Harvest House), I go into the symptoms of depression and the areas of self-help, outside help, and spiritual help. This simple study will bring understanding to all temperaments on the subject of depression and will be especially helpful to Perfect Melancholies.

REMEBER

Accentuate the positives.
Eliminate the negatives.

PROBLEM: *Perfect Melancholies Have Low Self-Images*

Solution 1: Search Out the Source of Your Insecurities

Because of their inborn negative inclinations, Perfect Melancholies focus their judgment most harshly upon themselves. They tend to feel insecure in social situations. They are usually attracted to Popular Sanguine mates who can do their conversing for them. I've met brilliant Perfect Melancholies, nationally known in their fields, who appeared to be terrified they might be asked to say a few words at a dinner party. Perfect Melancholies' low self-image often comes from criticism given them by their parents and teachers when they were young. Since Perfect Melancholies soak up negatives, people tend to put more on them. I've noticed in women's club work that presidents who let criticism get to them, get picked on. Those who don't let it bother them are left alone.

I have made up a self-image chart for women. It asks them their opinion of their hair, weight, eyes, talent, spirituality, and many other factors. After each woman writes her instant opinion of herself, I ask her to go back over the list and note where she first picked up this opinion. Was it her mother telling her she had terrible hair? Her father saying she wasn't very bright? Amazing insight comes to women as they do this simple exercise. They begin to realize why they have low self-images. I then have them evaluate whether their opinion is a valid one today, or whether it's a leftover. If it's valid, then we work out a schedule of improvement. If it is a myth, they ask the Lord to remove such fictional negatives from their minds. "Hear my prayer, O LORD, and let my cry [for help] come unto thee" (Ps. 102:1).

Solution 2: Listen for Evidence of "False Humility"

Because Perfect Melancholies have low self-images, they tend to seek praise in a subtle way that even they don't recognize in themselves. They say things such as: "I never do anything right; my hair is always a mess; I never know what to wear." In saying words such as these, they feel they are being humble, but in actuality each utterance is like waving a red flag saying, "I'm insecure." What Perfect Melancholies are actually doing is asking for a lift in their images and forcing us to give a compliment, which they may then reject.

REMEMBER

Perfect Melancholies have the greatest potential
for success. Don't be your own worst enemy.

PROBLEM: *Perfect Melancholies Procrastinate*
Solution 1: Get the "Right Things" Before Starting

Because Perfect Melancholies are perfectionists, they often refrain from starting certain projects because they are afraid they won't do them right. While Peaceful Phlegmatics procrastinate in hopes they won't have to do it, Perfect Melancholies hold back because they have to do it perfectly.

When we lived in Connecticut, Fred decided to put in a Perfect Melancholy music system. As a start, he cut a big hole in a living room wall and set a speaker into it. The turntable was hidden in a closet, but the speaker became the focal point of the room and ruined the decor. I tried to get him to put something—anything—over this black hole, but he had to wait until he found the "right thing." I found a picture I could hang over it, but the gouged plaster showed on the sides—plus Fred wouldn't let me leave it up since it distorted the sound. Every solution I suggested wasn't "right." I put the piano in front of the hole and piled hymn books on top, but that didn't work. I tried huge bouquets of flowers, but they only drew attention to the black circle behind them. Christmas was the best time of the year because a large, full tree covered the hole, and people were impressed with music coming out through the tinsel. Two years later, when Fred admitted he might never find the right thing, I had a carpenter come in and build a cabinet over the hole. I discussed this with Fred several months before he could say, "I think that's the right thing." Perfect Melancholies, don't tease the rest of us with your brilliant projects until you've got the "right things" to carry them through quickly.

Solution 2: Don't Spend So Much Time Planning

One lady told me her husband did get all the right things before pouring a new patio. Bags of cement sat on the lawn killing the grass, and an old wheelbarrow reclined by the front door for months. Every time she complained he said he couldn't do the patio until he had a master plan for the whole yard. He is still designing the landscaping, and she has put geraniums in the wheelbarrow.

Arlene asked her husband for some simple bookshelves. He spent three months making sketches. Jackie's husband built a stand to hold his son's aquarium. She brought me four pages of actual blueprints he had made before he could begin construction.

If I ask Fred to hang a picture, he has to analyze the wall. Invariably, it's crooked and this revelation is depressing. He has to measure the height and width of the wall and the dimensions of the picture. He needs the right kind of nails and a small hammer, which is usually missing. I've learned that if I want a picture hung quickly, I grab the first nail I can find, and an old shoe, and whack the nail in where I think the picture should go. If it doesn't look right where I have the picture hung, I pull the nail out and move it over a few inches. After a few quick drives, I get it in the right spot. When we moved the last time, Fred took the pictures down and was distraught that behind every scene was a series of holes that he had to plaster before we could sell the house.

REMEMBER

If Perfect Melancholies didn't spend so much time
in planning, they wouldn't force the rest of us
incompetents to go ahead without preparation
and so botch up intricate work!

PROBLEM: *Perfect Melancholies Put Unrealistic Demands on Others*

Solution 1: Relax Your Standards

Because Perfect Melancholies have high standards they do everything to perfection, but when they impose their standards on others, this trait becomes a weakness.

One Popular Sanguine girl stated at a seminar, "I have never done one thing since we got married that my Perfect Melancholy husband didn't correct. When I die I'll have to come back and do it over again, because I'll never get it right the first time."

When I held a seminar in Palm Springs, a very elegant Perfect Melancholy lady came up to talk with me. "I've never heard of the temperaments before, and I'm wondering if this could explain what's wrong with my peculiar child."

She then told about the "normal" standards in her home. She, her husband, and one son were Perfect Melancholies, and they kept everything just right. She placed the magazines on the coffee table in a perfect row, with each one down far enough to expose the name of the one under it. The magazines were exactly two inches from the edge of the table, and they were always the current issues. No one could read a magazine until the next issue came, so they would always look fresh and crisp. One day her "peculiar son" (who was ten) walked into the living room, pushed all the magazines onto the floor, grabbed one, ripped the cover off, crumpled it up, and threw it at her feet. She had been so distraught at this abnormal behavior that she had made an appointment for her son with a child psychiatrist.

As we discussed the problem, I shared with her that while the Perfect Melancholy felt having everything "just so" was normal, this kind of constant pressure was enough to drive a Popular Sanguine child wild. The boy couldn't take this dollhouse existence any longer. Knowing the temperaments is such a help in dealing with others. The lady had high standards that were great for her and the other two Perfect Melancholies, but put upon a Popular Sanguine they were impossible. As she understood this she said, "I thought he was a mental case."

"He will be if you keep this up," I replied.

Solution 2: Be Grateful You Understand Your Temperament

The study of the temperaments is of great value to Perfect Melancholies. As they can begin to understand why others behave and react differently, they can start to work on their relationships with family and friends in a positive way.

Many Perfect Melancholies feel there is something wrong with them because they are not lighthearted and jovial as others seem to be. People tell them to cheer up and loosen up, and they withdraw instead. So many Perfect Melancholies have told me what a burden was lifted from their minds when they realized they were not mentally ill, but one of four basic temperaments.

Linda Schreiber wrote from Laguna:

It will be difficult to put into words how valuable the section on the temperaments was to me. I find it hard to believe that this is as old as Hippocrates, and yet this is the first time I've ever been exposed to it. I am a true Perfect Melancholy and knowing about the temperaments solved so many problems in my own mind. I can't tell you how many times I've been really hurt by friends. Now I can easily see that most of my friends are Popular Sanguines. They don't mean to hurt me, but I'm just too sensitive for their ways. The thing that throws me is that it is so simple now that I can see the total picture. I don't think that I have any friends or even relatives, that are Perfect Melancholies. My feelings were always so strong compared to everyone else that I was beginning to think I had severe emotional problems! It was just like a weight being lifted to learn that I'm not so different but just one of four basic temperaments!

REMEMBER

Not everything in life can be perfect, so relax.

However! The Word of God reminds us:

> *Strive for perfection; listen to my appeals; agree with one another; live in peace . . .*

2 Corinthians 13:11 GNB

CHAPTER 10

Let's Tone Down Powerful Choleric

As Popular Sanguines see their weaknesses as trivial, and Perfect Melancholies see them as real and hopeless, Powerful Cholerics refuse to believe there is anything about them that could be offensive. Because of their basic premise that they are always right, they naturally can't see that they could possibly be wrong.

Right from the time they are little children, Powerful Cholerics must win in every situation, and they will find a way not to lose face.

Powerful Choleric Bryan, five years old, appeared ready to go to a birthday party wearing old Reeboks. His mother instructed him to go back to his room and put on his dress-up shoes.

"I hate those shoes," he said clearly. His Powerful Choleric mother replied, "I don't care whether you like them or not. Just put them on."

"I won't wear the brown shoes," Bryan stated.

"Then you won't go to the party!"

Bryan was faced with a problem. He wanted to go, but he didn't want to wear the brown shoes. His Powerful Choleric nature wouldn't allow him to give in and yet his mother was driving the car, and he knew from experience that she meant what she said.

He stood momentarily baffled and then came up with a Powerful Choleric solution that allowed him to save face. "I'll put the brown shoes on, but when I come home from the party, I will throw them in the trash and I will never wear them again!"

Byran felt he had the victory!

Mr. No-Fault

During the break at a marriage seminar one evening, a Powerful Choleric man came charging up the aisle, waving his temperament papers in the air.

"I have all of these strengths and none of the weaknesses," he shouted. Behind him was a little Peaceful Phlegmatic wife, shaking her head *no* but not daring to utter a word.

"Furthermore," he said, "these things aren't even weaknesses."

"What do you mean?" I asked.

"Well, look at this word *impatience*. I would never get impatient if everybody would do what I told them to when I told them to do it!" He pounded the lectern for Powerful Choleric emphasis, and in words only a Powerful Choleric can say with a straight face, he concluded, "Impatience is not a weakness in me; it is a fault in others."

Right there is the heart of the Powerful Choleric problem, and the reason they don't try to improve. They are always able to rationalize why the weakness is not *theirs* but is a fault in others. If Powerful Choleric can ever be convinced of his abrasive nature, he will be the quickest of all to improve, because he is goal oriented and must prove to himself that he can conquer anything if he sets his mind to it.

PROBLEM: Powerful Cholerics Are Compulsive Workers

Solution 1: Learn to Relax

Powerful Choleric is a great worker and can accomplish more than any other temperament, but on the negative side, he just can't relax. He goes full steam ahead so long that he can't quite throw the switch and turn himself off. Since Fred and I are both partially Powerful Choleric, you can imagine the activity we generate. If we sit down, we feel guilty. Life was made for constant achievements and production.

> Every house was made to be changed.
> Every meal could be better.
> Every drawer could be neater.
> Every job could be done faster.

The Powerful Choleric in us makes us go, go, go. Don't ever sit down if there's something you can stand up and do!

I once was telling a Peaceful Phlegmatic friend how I have to force myself to rest, and the only way I can take a nap is if I consider sleeping as a step to the goal of good health.

"All the time I'm resting," I explained, "I'm planning what I'm going to do as soon as I get up."

"That's funny," she said. "All the time you're down, you're wishing you were up. With me it's just the opposite. All the time I'm up, I'm wishing I were lying down."

We both laughed as we realized the extreme differences in the Powerful Choleric who loves to work and the Peaceful Phlegmatic who loves to rest.

Last year Fred and I decided we badly needed a rest. My brother Ron suggested an island in the Bahamas that is so remote we would be forced to relax. We flew off to this paradise where we planned to do nothing but rest.

We missed breakfast the first day. (By the time we got down the staff had left!) After breakfast on the second day, we went out to investigate the long, slim island. We were right in the center, and we found there were only two things to do: walk to the right or walk to the left. By lunchtime we'd done both.

After lunch Fred and I went to our room and sat on the edge of the twin beds. Fred took out a clipboard and legal pad and said, "I think it's about time we got this vacation organized. We'd better go to breakfast early before the staff quits. We'll take our time and get into our bathing suits at 9:30 A.M. We'll then walk to the left. Since we have to get a tan we'll lie on the beach until 11:00 A.M., when we'll come back to the room to dress for lunch."

I nodded along as Fred wrote down our schedule accounting for every minute, up to a 3:00 P.M. walk to the right.

At this point I realized what we were doing. The Powerful Cholerics in need of a rest were planning out each day, so that we wouldn't waste our vacation. Even though we knew why we had chosen a quiet place, it was so contrary to our natures to relax that we were planning how to make the most of our time!

Powerful Cholerics must realize they are heart-attack candidates, and they must learn to relax. I force myself to rest, and I discipline myself to go to bed at a decent hour when I'm traveling. Although parties may go on, I say good night and retire.

Powerful Choleric will never be lazy, but he must realize he doesn't have to work all the time.

Solution 2: Read *When I Relax I Feel Guilty*

It is hard for Powerful Cholerics to take it easy. Tim Hansel has written a book custom-tailored for Powerful Cholerics, *When I Relax I Feel Guilty* (David C. Cook). He says, "Leisure has always been difficult for me to incorporate into my life. I have rarely been accused of working too little. My problem has been just the opposite. I figured if it were good to work ten hours it would be even better to work fourteen."

Then he challenges other workaholics. "Is it possible that your days are hurrying by so fast that you don't fully taste them anymore? Are *play* and *rest* foreign words in your living vocabulary? When was the last time you flew a kite, went for a bike ride, or made something with your hands? When was the last time you caught yourself enjoying life so deeply that you couldn't quite get the smile off your face? Chances are, it's been too long."

Tim spoke to Fred and me. He showed us we didn't have to organize our vacations or push our children. We could relax and not feel guilty. As Fred and I have laid this weakness out in the open, we have begun to have fun together. I've stopped pushing him to do yard work each weekend, and I no longer feel it's a sin if my house isn't in museum condition at all times.

Powerful Cholerics have to learn to relax. Try it—you might like it!

Solution 3: Take the Pressure off Others

Powerful Choleric's amazing capacity for work is at once an asset and a liability. From a business point of view, the love for progress and achievement makes Powerful Choleric the king of the road. Whether male or female, Powerful Choleric is raring to go and running for the goal. Powerful Choleric can accomplish more in a shorter time than any other temperament. The average Popular Sanguine needs some of the Powerful Choleric drive to get anything done, and Perfect Melancholy needs the Powerful Choleric compulsion to get him from the analysis to the actual work. Peaceful Phlegmatic, who would rather watch than work, has to push himself to set goals that are inherent in Powerful Choleric. This drive for achievement comes prepackaged in Powerful Choleric and other temperaments wilt before his hot pursuit of the prize.

Powerful Choleric's single-mindedness of purpose, allowing nothing to stand in his way, is what makes him accomplish far more than other temperaments, but this drive can be wearing on others.

Dorothy Shula says of husband, Don, coach of the Miami Dolphins, "I'm fairly confident that if I died tomorrow, Don would find a way to preserve me until the season was over and he had time for a nice funeral."

I would rather work than do anything else. Recently on a trip to Phoenix, Marita and I had a blowout on her car and had to bump along to a gas station. I had been working on the outlines and notes for my Speakers' Training Seminar all the way over and was deep in my work. When we got to the garage, I got out of the car with all the folders in my arms and laid them out in numerical order on the hood of the car while the back was being jacked up. All of a sudden, I saw what I was doing. I was so involved in my organization that I couldn't stop working, and here I was in a strange garage spreading manila folders all over the car while mechanics worked around me. I couldn't take a rest; I had a compulsion to work.

Powerful Cholerics have to realize that even though we have work, our compulsion for accomplishment puts a terrible pressure on those around us. They are made to feel that if they aren't driving every minute, they're second-class citizens. Dorothy Shula must feel something less than a Dolphin. I put pressure on those around me. Powerful Cholerics must work at not becoming workaholics so people can enjoy being with them and not have to run away to keep from having a nervous breakdown.

Solution 4: **Plan Leisure Activity**

Because Powerful Choleric loves to work even on vacation, other Powerful Cholerics have come up with a new occupation—that of

Leisure Time Counselors. It's only logical that we Powerful Cholerics make a business of our pleasure and hire someone to find fun for us! In an article "They'll Help Organize Your Leisure Time" (*Parade*, February 25, 1979), Dr. Chester McDowell, Leisure Lifestyle Consultant, is quoted as saying about us workaholics, "They erect all sorts of barriers that prevent them from enjoying themselves and they feel guilty about leisure. We help break down the barriers."

Research done on workaholics shows they don't have the need for diversion that other temperaments do, and they love their work. They do not have any more psychological problems than others—a fact that appears to surprise the researchers who are, no doubt, Perfect Melancholies looking for deep and hidden neuroses.

Powerful Cholerics just like to work.

In an article, "Is Your Fun Too Much Work?" (*Parade*, October 11, 1981), Madelyn Carlisle asks, "Is your recreation wrecking you? Is it boring you when what you need is stimulation? Is it making you tense when what you seek is relaxation?" She then points out how important it is for everyone to plan some quiet time if their job is active, or some exercise if their job is sedentary. Powerful Cholerics should plan some leisure activity.

REMEMBER

You can relax and not feel guilty.

PROBLEM: *Powerful Cholerics Must Be in Control*

Solution 1: Respond to Other Leadership

In dealing with extreme Powerful Cholerics, I have found they are comfortable only when in control positions. Marita dated an exceptionally Powerful Choleric young man who was continental and charming. When we would meet him in his area, he would treat us royally, giving expensive pens for table gifts, and tipping the waitress heavily for extra service. When we hosted him in our home, he was ill at ease and not so gracious. As we analyzed this contrast in behavior, we realized he was insecure when not in control.

Powerful Choleric must learn to adapt to social situations and try to relax when he is not in charge. He must let others make decisions and organize functions. He must respond to events he didn't plan and leadership not of his own choosing.

Solution 2: Don't Look Down on "The Dummies"

One of the most dramatic weaknesses of Powerful Choleric is his firm conviction that he is right and those who don't see things his way are wrong. He always knows how to do everything the quickest and the best, and he tells you so. If you don't happen to respond, you are at fault. Powerful Choleric spends much of his time standing on the top of the world, looking down at what he often calls the "dummies of life." This superior attitude can do psychological damage to those under Powerful Choleric's domain.

Because Powerful Choleric values strength in himself, he looks down with little mercy on weaknesses in others. He can't tolerate sick people, and as one friend told me of her Powerful Choleric husband, "When I'm sick he puts me in bed. He says, 'Come out when you're well' and shuts the door."

A Powerful Choleric speaker I recently met told me, "I hate insecure people; I just want to shake them." Not being able to stand weaknesses in others is a major weakness in Powerful Cholerics. They just don't understand people who aren't like them and think all others are weak or stupid. It is difficult for the Powerful Choleric to comprehend that not everyone is going to respond to his strong leadership. He expects everyone to get motivated by his programs and inspired by his ideas.

When a Powerful Choleric understands the temperaments, he can tailor his leadership to fit the variety of individuals. When he does not know the temperaments he rallies other Powerful Cholerics to his principles and lets "the dummies" fall by the wayside.

Solution 3: Stop Manipulating

Powerful Choleric has an amazing way of getting others to do things without realizing how they were conned. While Popular Sanguine charms others into waiting on him, Powerful Choleric manipulates. Naturally, a Popular Sanguine/Powerful Choleric combination manipulates in such a charming manner, you think you dreamed up the idea yourself.

When Marita was twelve years old, she wanted to go on a daylong "Jesus March," and I was resisting her request until I received this note:

> Let marita
> go on the Jesus
> Hike If you are wonder-
> ing who is spe talking
> this is the Lord. I will be with
> her and protect her she will
> be able to work for you Saterday
> and your work will be blessed I
> if you allow her to go
>   I know you will
> Let marita go,
>   God

How can one oppose the will of God?

Lauren, who is more Powerful Choleric than Marita, is a master manipulator. One day she posed a hypothetical question to me. Her Schnauzer dog, Monie, was in heat, and Lauren asked, "If you were going to have one of Monie's next puppies, would you prefer I bred her to this great champion I found in Palm Springs, or just to the plain Schnauzer down the street?" I hesitated to answer this question, because I definitely did not want anything that had to be fed or mopped up after. "If I were going to have one (which I'm not), I would definitely want one from a champion versus a plain dog down the street."

Quickly Lauren agreed. "I knew you'd see it my way. Now on Wednesday, when she must be bred, I will need three hundred and fifty dollars, and you could cover this in one of two ways. You could either give me the money outright, or I could retain the stud fee rights to your puppy, which would make up the difference within a few years."

I sat dumbfounded. Within two minutes, I had gone from not wanting a puppy under any circumstances to breeding Schnauzers without even getting a stud fee!

Once I regained my composure my Powerful Choleric nature firmly turned down this promising offer, and I felt I had come out on top. But Powerful Cholerics never give up. Lauren bred Monie with the plain dog down the street and gave me a tiny puppy in a box for Christmas.

While these two family stories are humorous, most of Powerful Choleric's schemes are not so funny. Even though Powerful Choleric seems to get away with his manipulations at the moment, later, when people reflect upon what's happened, they resent being conned. To keep friends and business associates for any period of time, Powerful Choleric must stop manipulating and become open with others. Powerful Cholerics resist this approach, because much of the joys of triumph are these very scheming conquests. If Powerful Cholerics could only see what an unappealing trait manipulation is, they might consider changing.

REMEMBER

Stop manipulating others and
looking down on "the dummies."

PROBLEM: *Powerful Cholerics Don't Know How to Handle People*

Solution 1: Practice Patience

I love the message in James 1:2, 3: "Is your life full of difficulties and temptations? Then be happy, for when the way is rough, your patience has a chance to grow. So let it grow, and don't try to squirm out of your problems" (TLB). What a great Scripture for Powerful Cholerics who want everything done their way *now*, and who try to squirm out of anything that isn't positive. Powerful Cholerics are impatient by nature, but this weakness can be overcome, once they realize it is a problem.

Since Powerful Cholerics can accomplish more in a shorter time than any other temperament, it is very hard for them to understand why others can't keep up with them. They feel that quiet people must be stupid and nonaggressive people must be weak. From a position of strength and self-confidence, they judge others to be somehow part of an inferior race.

The greatest value a Powerful Choleric can receive from this study of temperaments is to realize his ability to accomplish and achieve is often a handicap in personal relationships. No one likes a bossy, impatient person who makes him feel insecure. If only Powerful Choleric could let his mind dwell, even momentarily, on the possibility that he might be abrasive to others, he could modify his behavior quickly and really be the great leader he already thinks he is.

Solution 2: **Keep Advice Until Asked**

Because Powerful Choleric has a compulsion to correct wrongs, he assumes everyone with a problem would love his solution. He feels led to give directions to everyone who needs help, whether or not he has been asked. Our friend John was driving down the hill from the mountains. He noticed the truck in front of him was "dog walking." That is, listing slightly to one side. Since the truck looked new, John assumed the man had bought a defective truck and would welcome his advice. He drove up beside the truck and started waving at the man to pull over. The man looked and then chose to ignore John, who became insistent by blowing his horn and pointing to the side of the road. Finally the man gave up and pulled over. John explained to the puzzled man, "Your truck is dog walking."

"It's *what?*"

"It's dog walking. That means you have a bent frame. It must have been dropped in shipment. You take this truck right back to the dealer. They shouldn't get away with that!"

After having given his directions, he left the man standing, dejected, by his truck. John drove off pleased with what a great help he'd been. Not everyone responds with joy to the Powerful Choleric's helpful suggestions.

Solution 3: **Tone Down Your Approach**

In a survey I took at a Personality Plus seminar on what traits people disliked most in others, the winner was *bossy*. No one liked bossy people. I asked them to write a second list of what negative traits *they* had, and not one of them was bossy. Isn't it amazing how we dislike bossy people, and yet not one of us is bossy. The obvious conclusion is that over-bearing people don't see themselves as others see them. They feel they are being helpful and others should be grateful for their instructions.

Because Powerful Choleric thinks so quickly and knows what's right, he says what comes to his mind, without worrying about how people will take it. He is more concerned with getting things done than with the feelings of others. He feels he's helping the cause, but those in his way may look at him as *bossy*.

Powerful Cholerics are not only bossy orally, they are great at writing notes of instruction. One day my Popular Sanguine friend Peggy came over with a clutch of papers in her hand. She was obviously upset as she shoved them at me and said, "Look at what my mother wrote to me! I was using her house while she was away and I was moving, and just look at these notes!" The first paper said:

Peggy, return my <u>red Dansk pot</u>!

(Powerful Cholerics love to underline for emphasis and use exclamation points to show they mean business.)
The second note said:

Peg,
Please <u>remember</u> to turn my furnace off before you leave as it runs up the BILL!!

The third had been taped over the washing machine with two Band-Aids.

Peg,
Turn off the two faucets after washing. If left on, water can leak out all over into the playroom. Also empty fuzz out of the dryer catcher <u>each time</u>!

Since Peggy is Popular Sanguine, she paid no attention to the notes. One day her mother had come by unexpectedly and found the place a mess. She had pinned the final note:

Peg,
I do <u>not</u> like the way I found my house when I returned.

You did not find my broiler dirty (like it was left), nor did you find our burglar alarm off—that is why we have it to protect our property.

<u>I'm very mad</u> as you can well tell!

<u>If</u> you use our home again <u>leave</u> it as <u>you found it</u>.

Love, Mother

While Peggy was upset, I was thrilled with the notes and asked if I could keep them. They are perfect examples of Powerful Choleric instructions, which they feel are justified (and others feel are bossy).

Solution 4: **Stop Arguing and Causing Trouble**

Because Powerful Choleric knows he's right, he loves to lead the confused, insecure public into battle—and then win triumphantly. Baiting "the dummies" and proving them wrong becomes a challenging hobby for Powerful Choleric.

Fred's brother Steve used to study "Words Commonly Mispronounced" in the *Reader's Digest*, carry the ripped-out pages in his wallet, and then wait for some innocent soul to make a mistake. Sooner or later someone would fall into the trap, and he would pounce upon that person with glee and say, "I think you will find that you have mispronounced that word." The victim would stammer as Steve pulled the proof from his wallet, pointed out the correction, and left the person devastated. Only Powerful Cholerics enjoy this ego game of shooting down the pigeons.

Powerful Cholerics love controversy and arguments and whether they play it for fun or for serious, this stirring up problems is an extremely negative characteristic.

REMEMBER

No one likes an impatient, bossy troublemaker.

PROBLEM: *Powerful Cholerics Are Right but Unpopular*
Solution 1: **Let Someone Else Be Right**

It is very difficult to counsel Powerful Choleric because he can always prove why what he did was right. Since he is perfect, if it weren't the correct thing to do, he would not have done it. Powerful Choleric just can't be wrong. He cannot admit to his inner self that he just might possibly be at fault. This unbending opinion makes dealing with Powerful Choleric close to impossible at times.

My brother Ron told me of an adventure he had with a Powerful Choleric optometrist. He wanted to have a pair of bifocal sunglasses made for his wife. He went to the man who had her prescription and told him what he had in mind. The man countered, "That's impossible." My brother, being Powerful Choleric himself, would not give in easily and he pursued his purpose.

"You don't understand what I'm saying: I want regular sunglasses with her reading prescription on the bottom, so she can look at a magazine while at the pool."

The man countered with another "That's impossible."

My brother continued making logical explanations, and the optometrist refused to budge. Ron finally took the prescription from the man's hand and said, "I'll go somewhere else and have this filled."

Not to be outdone, the man called to Ron on the way out, "If you take that somewhere else and they fill it the way you want it, they're wrong!"

What a classic example of the Powerful Choleric who knows he's right.

Solution 2: **Learn to Apologize**

Because Powerful Choleric knows everything and is convinced he's always right, he cannot imagine he should ever apologize. He looks at

"I'm sorry" as a sign of weakness and avoids its expression as he would a disease. We had a Powerful Choleric young man live with us for a year, and during that time he felt free to criticize us, but never saw that *he* was any problem. One morning he came out after breakfast was over and started to look for some cold cereal. He took out the one box I had and told me bluntly, "You know I don't like this kind of cereal. Can't you ever have anything I like?" He threw the box on the counter and stormed out without eating. Later, young Fred, who was twelve at the time and had witnessed the rejection of Brand *X*, came up to me quietly in his Perfect Melancholy sensitivity and said, "I want to apologize for Robert. He wasn't very nice to you about the cereal, but I know he'll never say he was sorry."

Fred was right. Robert never apologized, and when he referred to the situation, he called it "the unfortunate misunderstanding you and I had over the cereal." Powerful Choleric just can't face the facts and say, "I'm sorry."

I got on a plane at Palm Springs, and an irate Powerful Choleric man sat down beside me. "Those idiots made me go through the security gate a second time, when all I did was go out to buy a magazine. I told them if I passed once, there was no point in doing it again, but they made me go through anyway." He was furious, so I didn't bother to give any opposing views. It is so difficult to counsel or reason with Powerful Cholerics because they know everything, can always place the blame on others, and can rationalize away any fault on their part.

Solution 3: **Admit You Have Some Faults**

Since Powerful Choleric has the greatest potential as a leader for the greatest causes, he should gain the most from the study of the temperaments. He should be able to take his dynamic strengths of quick, decisive action and move to eradicate his sins of conceit and impatience.

But Powerful Choleric is his own worst enemy. He has tattooed the word *strength* on his right arm, and he thinks the word *weakness* belongs only to others. It is this refusal to look at any possible fault in his own makeup that keeps Powerful Choleric from achieving the heights within his grasp.

Shakespeare often wrote of the great hero marred by a tragic flaw. In the Powerful Choleric the tragic flaw is his inability to see that he has any. He is more interested in being right than being popular, and when he takes a stand he is inflexible.

REMEMBER

If only the Powerful Choleric would open his mind
to examine his weaknesses and admit he had a few,
he could become the perfect person he thinks he is.

And don't forget, Powerful Choleric:

If we confess our sins, he is faithful and just to forgive us our sins, and to cleanse us from all unrighteousness.

1 John 1:9

CHAPTER **11**

Let's Motivate
Peaceful Phlegmatic

As with each temperament, the types of strengths have corresponding weaknesses. Peaceful Phlegmatics have low-key strengths, so they have low-key weaknesses. Where Powerful Choleric lays his strengths right out before you, so his faults are obvious and out in the open; the Peaceful Phlegmatic keeps both his best and his worst under wraps. Many Peaceful Phlegmatics can't imagine they could possibly be offensive because they are so quiet and kind. It is difficult to communicate with them in a seminar for they are usually sleepy by the time I get to their section.

One day as I was shopping for Peaceful Phlegmatic chairs—ones that are quiet and unobtrusive and will blend with any decor—the thought came to me: *Peaceful Phlegmatic's greatest strength is his lack of obvious weaknesses.* Peaceful Phlegmatic doesn't have temper tantrums, sink into depressions, or spin his wheels noisily. He just stays unenthusiastic, worries quietly, and can't make decisions. Hardly faults obvious enough to demand correction.

PROBLEM: *Peaceful Phlegmatics Are Not Exciting*
Solution: **Try to Get Enthused**

One of the most annoying weaknesses of Peaceful Phlegmatic is his inability to get enthused over anything. I once asked Don Air Force (One of Lauren's boyfriends) if he ever got excited, and after thinking for several seconds, he replied, "I can't remember anything in life that was worth getting excited about."

131

While this weakness is not a loud, glaring one, it is extremely discouraging for the mate to have a partner who doesn't get enthused over his dynamic plans. The one bounces in, full of great thoughts for the weekend, and Peaceful Phlegmatic says, "That doesn't sound like much fun. Why bother going? I'd just rather stay home." This drops the creative partner to a low, and no matter what happens this weekend, one of them is unhappy.

The Powerful Choleric woman is attracted to the Peaceful Phlegmatic man because he has that cool detached look that is somehow appealing in its quiet way. The Powerful Choleric man chooses the Peaceful Phlegmatic woman because she has a soft, gentle spirit and needs to be protected from the cruel, hard world.

After the wedding Powerful Cholerics set their goals in order and nail up their edicts, expecting instant enthusiasm. When Peaceful Phlegmatic replies, "I couldn't care less," Powerful Choleric is crestfallen, and tries to come up with more dynamic ideas that will demand response. Little does Powerful Choleric know, the more grandiose the scheme, the more frightened and less excited Peaceful Phlegmatic will be.

I've spent most of my life trying to get my mother turned on to some of my accomplishments. When I wrote my first book I thought: *Now I have done something she'll get enthused about. Not every daughter has written a book. She'll love it! I've even dedicated it to her. I can't miss!*

I handed her the book and showed her the dedication. I then waited for her to see herself in print and be filled with joy. No reaction. She turned the page. I watched. She never changed her expression in the days she took to read it, and when she was finished, she closed the book and looked out the window. I could hardly wait for her comments, but they did not come. Finally I said to Lauren, "Ask Grammie how she liked my book." She did, and my mother replied, "It sure was a book."

Once Peaceful Phlegmatics find they can upset others by their refusal to get enthused, they use this ability as a quiet form of control and chuckle under their breath at the antics the rest of us go through, trying to elicit excitement. After a weekend retreat where there were several speakers, the chairman asked a Peaceful Phlegmatic lady which speaker she liked best. She meditated a moment and then said, "I think it will take time to know."

Another was asked "Would you attend again?" The Peaceful Phlegmatic answer was, "Possibly, or more likely I would recommend it to others and have them attend."

A young Popular Sanguine girl shared at a seminar, "My husband is so Peaceful Phlegmatic he even falls asleep during arguments."

Linda said, "Living with my husband is like being a talk-show host. He comes home and sits silently. I lean over and say, 'And what's your name, honey?' If I can pull anything out of him at all, I'm lucky." Peaceful Phlegmatics just don't get very excited about anything.

Putting two Peaceful Phlegmatics together in marriage is a sure way to avoid problems and excitement. The couples I have known with this combination have gotten along well and kept life on the Peaceful Phlegmatic "even keel," but they have frequently expressed, "Frankly, we're bored."

A young girl told me, "We've been married one year and we've run out of anything to say or do." One said, "Each night I ask him, 'What do you feel like doing?' He answers, 'I don't care, what do you want to do?' Since neither one of us can decide, we don't do much of anything."

Another lady explained, "We get along fine. I ask him to hang a picture; he says yes and forgets. I'm so Peaceful Phlegmatic I don't care." A man overhearing this comment added, "We laid pictures out on the floor in our dining room when we first moved into the house a year ago. We're going to hang them sometime, but it doesn't ever seem urgent."

The Peaceful Phlegmatic chairman of one of our seminars reported, "My wife and I are both Peaceful Phlegmatic, and each night when I get home she asks, 'What do you feel like eating?' and I reply, 'What do you have?' She says, 'Not much! How about TV dinners?' I nod and we both go to the freezer and stand with the door open trying to decide which variety to choose."

REMEMBER

Get enthused. Start with once a month
and work up from there.

PROBLEM: *Peaceful Phlegmatics Resist Change*

Solution: Try Something New

One night Lee's Peaceful Phlegmatic husband, Pete, came home and said, "Get dressed, I'm taking you out." She was so excited and she began to think of what she'd wear. She asked, "Where are you taking me?" Pete answered, "To Montgomery Ward to buy trash cans." I asked her how she reacted to such a thought and she replied, "I got dressed and went. It was the most exciting thing he'd thought of in months."

Unfortunately, this incident is the norm with many Peaceful Phlegmatics. They have no need of entertainment and assume no one else does either. I saw a cartoon that showed a Peaceful Phlegmatic man, lying on the floor next to a mousehole in the baseboards. He was holding a hammer in the air, ready to whack the first rodent who stuck his head out. His wife looked down at him and sighed, "Another exciting Saturday evening with Harry."

One Peaceful Phlegmatic man asked my advice on his dull marriage. When I gave him some new ideas, he countered, "I think I'll just pretend everything's all right—a change might be worse."

REMEMBER

Try your best to think of something new at least
once a week. Your partner deserves a change.

PROBLEM: *Peaceful Phlegmatics Seem Lazy*

Solution 1: Learn to Accept Responsibility for Your Life

Peaceful Phlegmatic in his most extreme form is very lazy and hopes by procrastinating to avoid any work at all. I chose one lady to be a chairperson in the Women's Club, and she asked, "Will I have to do anything?" She didn't mind the title, as long as it didn't involve work.

Jill was moving and the thought of it overwhelmed her. She asked her friends to help her pack, and for three months they talked about what day they'd come to help. At the appointed time, her Powerful Choleric friends came ready to work. Jill had on a dress, nylons, and high heels, giving an instant impression that she didn't plan on any heavy labor herself. Although it was the day before the movers were to arrive, Jill had no boxes or bags; she had packed nothing; the pictures were still on the walls; the sink was full of dirty dishes; and there were piles of laundry to get done.

One friend told me, "She expected us to do everything!"

If you do want others to do the work, at least be smart enough not to give them advice.

Peaceful Phlegmatic Phil sat comfortably in a chair by the fire while his Powerful Choleric wife was loading up the van for their skiing trip. At one point he looked up and commented, "If you'll take more out on each trip it won't take you so long." He wondered why she hit him over the head with a ski pole.

In our seminars, when it's time to divide into groups, the Peaceful Phlegmatics never know where to go and they turn to their mates in bewilderment. The partner (who is usually Powerful Choleric) comes up with a loving, "You're a Peaceful Phlegmatic, you dummy!" and the person shuffles off to find where the Peaceful Phlegmatic group went.

One Peaceful Phlegmatic dentist, when chosen to be chairman of the group, suggested, "Why don't we all close our eyes and meditate until the time is up?"

Another man agreed with "You can't improve on silence."

Solution 2: Don't Put Off Until Tomorrow What You Can Do Today

The problem of procrastination is prevalent with both Perfect Melancholies and Peaceful Phlegmatics, but for different reasons. Perfect Melancholy cannot start anything until he has the right equipment and feels he can do a perfect job; but Peaceful Phlegmatic postpones because underneath he doesn't want to do it. He tends to be lazy, and postponements keep him from making a decision to get to work. Peaceful Phlegmatic has a mañana complex: Never do today what you can put off until tomorrow.

At a baby shower for my daughter Lauren, the Peaceful Phlegmatics brought gifts that they hadn't quite gotten around to finishing yet.

The first was an adorable blue suit with a snap crotch, but upon inspection, we found straight pins where the snaps should have been. If the poor baby ever put his legs together, he'd be stabbed! The second was a needlepoint unicorn, without any background. Both girls expressed a sincere desire to finish their projects, and they both left the shower with their gifts in hand.

These two girls with their half-done presents were still far better than the Popular Sanguine who forgot what day it was and didn't come at all!

Solution 3: **Motivate Yourself**

Sharon's mind was like a game of pool. The colorful balls only rolled around when pushed, and had for years clustered cozily in a mesh bag, hanging securely in the corner.

It wasn't that she couldn't move; it was just too much like work. When properly motivated, she could pull a few balls out of the pocket and roll them around the fertile green, as long as the occasion demanded. When the pressure relaxed, she would clear the table and retreat to her net, until someone in exasperation would grab the colored balls, throw them across the green and cry, "*Move!*"

This simple little parable is typical of Peaceful Phlegmatic. It's not that they *can't* do the job; it's that they don't want to. One lady told me she had cut out at least four dresses, but it was just too much like work to sew them up. "If I ever need one for a special occasion, I'll do it."

While Peaceful Phlegmatics need direct motivation from others, they resent being pushed. This contradictory problem is a conflict in many homes where Peaceful Phlegmatic avoids doing the necessary chores; Powerful Choleric tells him what to do, and he resents the prodding.

Ruthee has a kitchen window that faces west, and each afternoon the California sun beats in, making the spot too hot to work. She asked Howard to put up a shade for her, but since he wasn't the one in the sun, he wasn't motivated. Finally Ruthee nailed up a big beach towel, which cuts down the heat but ruins the view. One day at a yard sale Ruthee found a pair of wooden shutters exactly the size of her window. She brought them home, but there was an instant problem: The shutters were unfinished. Howard was mildly enthused over the new shutters, and assured Ruthee he would antique them to match the cabinets.

That was four years ago and the shutters are still in various stages in the garage. When Ruthee asks about their progress, he gets offended and says he is "working on them." Ruthee's solution is to forget she ever bought the shutters and put up fresh towels with every season.

REMEMBER

You Peaceful Phlegmatics deserve to be henpecked if you can't motivate yourselves to responsible action.

PROBLEM: *Peaceful Phlegmatics Have a Quiet Will of Iron*

Solution: **Learn to Communicate Your Feelings**

Because Peaceful Phlegmatic appears to go along with the crowd, people are often surprised when they find a quiet will of iron at work under the placid exterior. As a composite example from many Powerful Choleric wives, the situation is this: Charlotte announces to Charlie on Monday morning, "We're going to Sally's house Saturday night."

Charlie gives a typical Peaceful Phlegmatic answer, "Ummm."

Charlotte, being a Powerful Choleric, takes any answer that isn't "absolutely not" as "yes," and assumes she and Charlie are agreed on Saturday night.

Every day that week Charlotte reminds Charlie, "Don't forget! Sally's house on Saturday night."

Charlie mumbles another "umm."

Saturday night comes. Charlotte gets dressed up, and Charlie sits in his recliner chair in a T-shirt. When he doesn't seem to move, Charlotte states clearly, "Hurry up and change your clothes. We're going to Sally's house."

Charlie gives the first complete sentence he's come up with all week. "I'm not going."

"You agreed with me about it all week."

"I didn't agree; I just didn't disagree." And Charlie doesn't go. Once the usually obliging Peaceful Phlegmatic makes a decision, you cannot change his mind.

I have learned from counseling Peaceful Phlegmatics that they appear to be content in their marriages. I ask if they have any complaints and they say, "Everything's just fine." The partner may be hysterical and threatening suicide, yet Peaceful Phlegmatic doesn't know what the problem is. He's innocent and won't communicate. The marriage may limp along for years with no open lines, until one day Peaceful Phlegmatic decides he's had it with the foolish woman, and he's going to leave. He doesn't bring the matter up for discussion; he just packs up and takes off. Once Peaceful Phlegmatic has made his move, there is little hope of changing him.

One man put it this way: "It took me twenty long years to get the courage to make this decision, and I'm sure not going to change my mind now."

The basic problem under this stubborn streak is that Peaceful Phlegmatic is unwilling to communicate. Since he always takes the path of least resistance and runs from controversy, he naturally finds it easier to keep quiet about his feelings rather than to open them up and take the chance of conflict.

By keeping his mouth shut Peaceful Phlegmatic stays out of trouble much of the time, but by hiding his feelings and refusing to communicate, he stifles any meaningful relationship with others.

REMEMBER

Open up before it's too late.
Don't hide your light under a bushel.

PROBLEM: *Peaceful Phlegmatics Appear Wishy-Washy*

Solution 1: Practice Making Decisions

Peaceful Phlegmatic's major fault is his apparent inability to make decisions. Powerful Choleric stands over him with a pot of boiling water and asks quickly, "Do you want coffee or tea?" The automatic answer is "I don't care." Peaceful Phlegmatic feels he is being agreeable and can't understand why Powerful Choleric pours the hot water over his head!

"I was only trying to make it easy for her."

On a flight out of Norfolk, Virginia, the flight attendant announced over the PA system that we had three choices of entrees for lunch. "You may have seafood Newburg, pepper steak, or lasagne. We do not have enough of each for everyone, so some of you at the end should think of a second choice."

She then turned immediately to the Peaceful Phlegmatic man who was in the first row with me and asked him, "Which entree would you like?" And he replied, "Whichever one you have left over." The flight attendant, being Powerful Choleric, said, "I don't have anything left over! You are the first person I've asked." She hovered over him, waiting for a decision. Then I spoke up and said, "I'll have the Newburg." He looked up and said, "I guess I'll have that one too."

Peaceful Phlegmatic's problem with making decisions is not that he is incompetent, but that he has made one great decision never to make any decisions. After all, if you don't make the decision, you're not held accountable for the outcome.

Peaceful Phlegmatic must practice making decisions and be willing to accept responsibility. The friends, workers, and mates of Peaceful Phlegmatic will rejoice when he is able to stand tall and be decisive. Say good-bye to the wishy-washy blues.

Solution 2: Learn to Say No

Peaceful Phlegmatics don't ever want to hurt anybody and they will buy something they don't even want in order not to say no. One Powerful Choleric told me, "Among the strengths of Peaceful Phlegmatics are their friendliness and their willingness to help. They never see a stranger. My fuzzy-bearlike husband, over the years, has brought home as old friends light-bulb salesmen, vacuum-cleaner salesmen, magazine salesmen, and an odd assortment of others, which my Choleric heart viewed with skeptical suspicion. A Peaceful Phlegmatic just can't say, 'No! No! No!'"

While Peaceful Phlegmatics do not get excited over the concept of temperaments, they do learn and gradually apply themselves. Since they have the least offensive weaknesses, they can change for the better very quickly—if they feel like it. Properly motivated, a Peaceful Phlegmatic can make himself get enthused over a few things a week, and this will truly please those who live or work with him. Since he is able to make decisions (but chooses not to), he can easily become decisive and lose his wishy-washy image when he sees how much this will help in his relationships.

REMEMBER

Learn to say no and practice making decisions.
Start with chocolate and vanilla if all thirty-one flavors
are just too much to cope with at once!

When you fear to make a decision, remember there is One who can help you.

For the Lord grants wisdom. . . . He shows how to distinguish right from wrong, how to find the right decision. . . .

Proverbs 2:6, 9 TLB

PART FOUR

Personality Principles

A Path to Improved Relations with Others

CHAPTER 12

Each Person Is a Unique Blend

As you have scored your own Personality Profile, you have found that you are unique. Probably no one else has ever come up with the exact blend of strengths and weaknesses you have. Most people have high totals in one temperament, with a secondary in another temperament and some scattered traits. Some people are evenly distributed, and these are usually Peaceful Phlegmatics, for they are the all-purpose people and also the ones who have the most difficulty in deciding their traits.

Let's look at some of the possible blends.

Natural Blends

As you can see by the chart, the Popular Sanguine/Powerful Choleric combination is a Natural Blend. They are both outgoing, optimistic, and outspoken. Popular Sanguine talks for pleasure, Powerful Choleric for business, but they both are verbal people. If you have this blend, you have the greatest potential for leadership. If you combine your two strengths, you have a person who can direct others and make them enjoy the work; a person who is fun loving yet can accomplish goals; a person with drive and determination, but who is not compulsive about achievements. This blend takes the extremes of work and play and produces a person who puts them in proper perspective. In the negative, such a blend could spawn a bossy individual who didn't know what he was talking about; an impulsive person who was running around in circles; or an impatient soul who was always interrupting and monopolizing conversation.

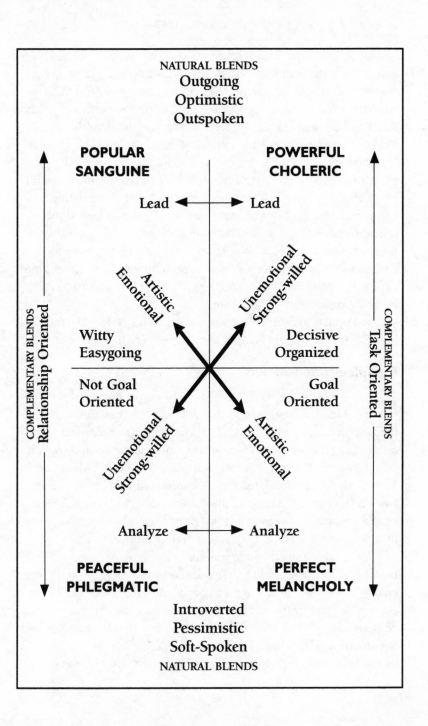

The other Natural Blend is the Perfect Melancholy/ Peaceful Phlegmatic. They are both introverted, pessimistic, and soft-spoken. They are more serious, they look into the depths of situations, and they don't want to be center stage. They follow Teddy Roosevelt's advice, "Speak softly and carry a big stick." Peaceful Phlegmatic lightens the depth of Perfect Melancholy, and the Perfect Melancholy pulls together the looseness of Peaceful Phlegmatic. This combination makes the greatest educators as Perfect Melancholies' love of study and research is brightened by Peaceful Phlegmatics' ability to get along with people and present material in a pleasant manner. They may have trouble in decision making because they both are slow in this area, and they both procrastinate. The best combination is one in which the evenness of Peaceful Phlegmatics keep Perfect Melancholy from dropping into depressions, and Perfect Melancholy's desire for perfection gets Peaceful Phlegmatic motivated to action.

The Popular Sanguine/Powerful Choleric and Perfect Melancholy/ Peaceful Phlegmatic are Natural Blends. They are blood brothers.

Complementary Blends

The Powerful Choleric/Perfect Melancholy temperament is a Complementary Blend, a combination that fits well together and completes the lacks in each other's natures. The Powerful Choleric/Perfect Melancholy makes the best business person because the combination of Powerful Choleric's leadership, drive, and goals with Perfect Melancholy's analytical, detail-conscious, schedule-oriented mind is unbeatable. Nothing is beyond the range of this combination, and they will be successful no matter how long it takes. If they set out to remake a mate, they will keep it up until they have a perfect product.

A lovely lady named Louise was confused about her own temperament, and as I asked what she was like in college, her whole face changed. She went from reserved to radiant as she told about being a cheerleader and being voted most likely to succeed. She realized she began to change under the direction of her boyfriend, whom she had later married. He, being a Powerful Choleric/Perfect Melancholy, had set out to perfect her. When she wrote him letters while he was in grad school, he would circle the misspelled words in red, and mail the letter back for her to study. When he came home, he would put her through a spelling bee. With good intentions and endless perseverance, he had remade a bouncing cheerleader into a serious, dignified actress who didn't quite know who she was.

Because this blend is decisive, organized, and goal oriented, Powerful Choleric/Perfect Melancholy has the most drive and determination and can hold tight onto a cause forever. Headed in a positive direction, the Powerful Choleric/Perfect Melancholies are the most successful, but carried to extremes, even their strengths become overbearing.

The other Complementary Blend is the Popular Sanguine/Peaceful Phlegmatic. Where the Powerful Choleric/Perfect Melancholy is work oriented, the Popular Sanguine/Peaceful Phlegmatic is inclined to take it easy and have fun. The combination of double portions of humor with easygoing natures makes the Popular Sanguine/Peaceful Phlegmatics the best friends possible. Their warm, relaxed natures are appealing and people love to be with them. Peaceful Phlegmatic tempers the ups and downs of Popular Sanguine, while Popular Sanguine personality brightens up Peaceful Phlegmatic. This blend is the best of all in dealing with people. They are good in personnel work, in being parents, and in civic leadership, because they have the engaging humor and personality of Popular Sanguine and the stability of Peaceful Phlegmatic. Unfortunately, the other side of the Popular Sanguine/Peaceful Phlegmatic shows them as lazy, without desire or direction to produce anything they can avoid, and very poor in handling money. As with each temperament blend there are exciting strengths and corresponding weaknesses.

Opposites

We have seen Natural Blends and Complementary Blends. Now we will look at the Opposites. There are obvious internal conflicts that the Popular Sanguine/Perfect Melancholy and the Powerful Choleric/Peaceful Phlegmatic can put into one person—the introvert and extrovert natures with the optimistic/pessimistic outlooks. The Popular Sanguine/Perfect Melancholy is the most emotional of the two, as one body tries to accommodate the little ups and downs of Popular Sanguine with the deeper, more prolonged traumas of Perfect Melancholy. This split personality can lead to emotional problems. The Popular Sanguine nature says, "Let's go and have more fun," and on the way, the Perfect Melancholy nature checks the progress.

One lady of this type told me of the anniversary party she planned for her parents. The Popular Sanguine part of her thought up great ideas including fancy invitations, a catered dinner, and an orchestra. Two days before the affair, her Perfect Melancholy part took over and said, "What in the world are you doing trying to put on this big party? Back out of this right this minute." She canceled the party and then was depressed for weeks over how she'd disappointed her parents.

To Work or Not to Work?

As we have done intensive case history studies of people who function in these extremes we have found that usually one of these is a learned response to the hurts of the past. We call these "Masks of Survival." Either the Perfect Melancholy child in order to seek parental attention put on a Popular Sanguine mask of popularity or the Popular Sanguine child, because of abuse or rejection, became depressed and put on the Perfect Melancholy mask of pain. Many children who are brought up in dysfunctional homes put on the Perfect Melancholy mask of perfection. "If only I could be perfect Daddy wouldn't hurt me, Mommy wouldn't yell at me." Whether it is from alcohol, drugs, rejection, sexual or emotional abuse, or extreme religious legalism, these dysfunctional homes breed masking of personality for the children. They don't know how to fight the system, so they tend to become whatever will help them survive.

As adults they appear to be split personalities and don't understand the extreme mood swings they suffer, to work or not to work . . . whether or not they are motivated to work. While the Powerful Choleric/Peaceful Phlegmatic opposite natures do not have the same emotional strains, they do have the major conflict of "to work or not to work." Peaceful Phlegmatic wants to take it easy, and Powerful Choleric feels guilty when not producing. This question usually resolves itself by dividing life into two segments—working hard at the job and tuning out at home.

Many times a Powerful Choleric will give his all at work, and then either be too exhausted to lift a finger at home, or not feel the home front is important enough to deserve his efforts. A Peaceful Phlegmatic may labor diligently on the job, where he may even seem Powerful Choleric because he is so motivated, and then relax completely at the end of the day.

If you seem to be in this blend, ask yourself whether you are a Powerful Choleric, playing low key at home, or a Peaceful Phlegmatic really motivated to work.

If these questions don't seem to bring satisfactory answers, perhaps you are wearing a mask of survival and don't realize that some of your childhood pain is still affecting your adult life. The Powerful Choleric child who is brought up in a home where his parents argue and fight sees quickly that the best thing for him to do is cover up his desire for control and keep quiet. The Powerful Choleric child who is allowed no part of the family decision making as it regards his clothes, his room, his pet, his school subjects, his career, and/or his choice of mate learns that he either has to fight for some control and be considered the "bad child" or he has to give up and accept authority until he can get out of the house. The Powerful Choleric child who is abused says to himself, "I'll keep quiet about it now; but when I get out of here, no one will ever control me again." Any one of these situations, or a combination, causes the Powerful Choleric child to put on the Peaceful Phlegmatic mask. As an adult he swings in and out of control and submission and doesn't understand why.

The Peaceful Phlegmatic child does not seek control and is usually the best behaved. Why would this child put on the mask of power and take charge? Only if he looks around his family situation, sees it spinning out of control, and says to himself "Somebody's got to do something to pull this place together." In a one-parent home, the responsibility of the missing person is often put upon one of the children. If this child is Peaceful Phlegmatic and he suddenly finds himself "the man of the house" he puts on the Powerful Choleric mask, strains his low-key nature, and takes control. As an adult he takes charge when he has to and drops into rest whenever he can. He feels perpetually exhausted and doesn't know why he feels torn up inside.

If you come out relatively even in either of these opposites, think about your feelings as a child and see if these explanations make sense to you. For further study read *Your Personality Tree*, especially the chapter on masking, and *Freeing Your Mind from Memories That Bind*.

If you come out "a little bit of everything" there are several possibilities. You took the test wrong; you didn't understand the words (see definitions on page 195); you are Peaceful Phlegmatic and have trouble making decisions; you are perfect and about to ascend; or you were so controlled, directed, or oppressed as a child that you can't get a true grasp on who you really are.

Whatever way you come out on the Personality Profile, remember it is not the label but the understanding of your own personality strengths and weaknesses that is important.

. . . I am fearfully and wonderfully made. . . .

Psalm 139:14

CHAPTER 13

We Don't Like to Be Fenced In

As I teach the concept of the temperaments in Personality Plus seminars, people sometimes ask me, "Are you trying to put us into little boxes?" As I have given this question much thought, I have come to the realization that we are already in our own little boxes. As we come to any experience in life, we bring our own structure along; we go only as far as we are comfortable. We don't climb over our portable walls and peek through the cracks before opening the gate.

Boxes from the Beginning

When we are first born, we are instantly put in our own little box. We are walled into our tiny space and wheeled over to a window, where fond relatives can look down into our box and view our helpless forms. We're wrapped into a tight bundle to be brought home and placed into our new box, a crib with bars around for our protection. For outings we are placed in a basket or strapped in an infant seat—even in the supermarket we're put inside a shopping cart for security. As we move up to bigger boxes, we're installed in a playpen, which keeps us in our place, and later, we're allowed to roam our room with a gate across the doorway. As we get daring, we're given the freedom of a fenced-in backyard. Each school grade has its room, and we settle in for a year, nestled in a protected space with a teacher.

We grow up in boxes, and even as we get out into the big world, we bring our walls along. When I had my first college roommate, we were both put into one box, but within days we had put up an invisible wall between us. We couldn't agree on bedspreads, wall posters, or housekeeping, so we put a strip of masking tape across the tile floor, and we each took our half of the room, turned our backs on the other, and created our own boxes where we felt secure.

The concept of the temperaments doesn't fence us in and put our feet in cement, but it does help us to see what kind of a box we're in, and how to move out of it. As we realize how imprisoned we are by our basic weaknesses, we can work to open the gate and dare to stray over to the yard next door. The comment we get the most frequently about the personalities is "This has set me free to be who I really am!" As we understand ourselves and become true to our own natures, we automatically develop a new acceptance for those people who don't see things our way and who wish to live in a style contrary to our perceptions.

When We Marry

When we think of how many years each of us spends in building his or her own box, and in decorating it with his or her own trophies, is it any wonder that when we marry someone with a different box, we don't automatically fit together?

We come into marriage from different spaces, and even on the honeymoon we wonder how soon the other will adjust to our structure. We may sleep in the same bed, but we keep fences around us.

One girl I counseled told me this story. Sylvia was an elegant Perfect Melancholy. Everything about her was perfect: her hair, her makeup, her nails. She was an airline flight attendant and had met her charming husband, Bud, on a cross-country flight. He had literally swept her off her feet with his Popular Sanguine personality and persuasive powers; within months they were married. Since she already had furnished and decorated a condominium on the West Coast, she felt it only natural to keep her home. Bud agreed, since he lived in an apartment with three other men and didn't have much furniture.

On Sylvia's first day back to work after the honeymoon, Bud explained he was going back to his apartment to pick up a few things. When Sylvia walked in that night she couldn't believe what she saw. Bud *had* moved in "a few things." There were ski posters nailed next to her Picasso prints; an ugly beanbag chair that looked like a dead elephant was slumped next to a Queen Anne sofa; and over the kitchen counter was a neon sign blinking the benefits of Budweiser Beer.

Sylvia loved the macho man in Bud, but she didn't know he would bring his box with him.

Understanding Our Basic Temperament Doesn't Fence Us In

It opens up a gate in our protective wall; it causes us to accept ourselves and others realistically, and it shows us how to anticipate problems and handle them before they happen. Think of the heartache we could have been saved *if* we'd dealt with collected trivia before it mounted up into a crisis! Understanding our own and others' temperaments gives us the ability to deal with situations *in the future* as we do now in retrospect. As we learn an individual's temperament, we can anticipate his reactions to different situations and have the available tools on hand to repair the damage before it starts.

Admit Your Weaknesses

The first step in any type of self-improvement is to find your areas of weakness and admit you have them. The refusal to examine our faults keeps us from doing anything positive about them. It is humbling to admit we've been doing something wrong for years, but it's the first step in growing up. Immature people blame their parents, their mates, their children, their friends, their circumstances, for why they have not become what they had hoped to be. A mature person examines himself, finds his faults, and gets to work on them.

It is important to look at our childhood pain and rejection in order to find out why we behave the way we do, but this search is not to place blame but to bring a measure of understanding and cause us to begin a healing process.

In Alcoholics Anonymous, each person has to stand up, give his first name, and say, "I am an alcoholic." Until a person can verbalize this admission, there can be no cure. We can't get over something we don't accept as a problem. If there were a Personality Anonymous, we would have to stand up and say:

> I'm a charming Popular Sanguine, but
>> I'm a compulsive talker.
> I'm a sensitive Perfect Melancholy, but
>> I get depressed easily.
> I'm a dynamic Powerful Choleric, but
>> I'm bossy and impatient.
> I'm an easygoing Peaceful Phlegmatic, but
>> I'm unenthusiastic.

From the point of admission we are headed in the right direction.

Let's Make a Personal Plan

Now that you understand the four basic temperaments and have scored yourself to find your custom blend of traits, you are ready to take steps to accentuate your positives and eliminate your negatives. Look over your Personality Profile.

Assess Your Strengths

Both Popular Sanguines and Powerful Cholerics see their strengths quickly and identify with them immediately, but often Perfect Melancholies and Peaceful Phlegmatics, because of their pessimistic natures, have to think awhile before accepting their positive qualities. Whichever your temperament, look over your Personality Profile realistically and decide which three strengths you feel are the most important in your relationships with others. List them here.

_____

_____

_____

(If you are doing this study with your family or a group, make this a time of discussion of each person's strengths, and encourage one another with sincere compliments.)

As you look at your strengths, thank God for the abilities He has given you and accept them. Those of you who tend to knock yourselves and say, "There's no good thing in me," change this attitude immediately. There is good in you. Your so-called false humility is unattractive, and forces others to lift you up constantly. This need is wearing on the others, tends to make them avoid you, and is an unnecessary crutch for a low self-image. You don't need to feel worthless ever again. You have been given both strengths and weaknesses. God created you just a "little lower than the angels," and He didn't intend that you waste any time in self-abnegation.

Look at the three strengths you have chosen. Thank God for them, and never forget you have worth. Are you using these abilities to their very fullest? As I teach at Personality Plus seminars and each person lists his talents, the participants are always amazed at what sources of strengths they are not using. So many have abilities lying dormant and talents untapped.

Some are still limping along because they were told as children: You'll never make it, you don't have any talent, you ruin everything you touch. Throw those past hurts away today and begin to function in all of your strengths.

Evaluate Your Weaknesses

As Perfect Melancholies and Peaceful Phlegmatics may have difficulty in relating to their strengths, so Popular Sanguines and Powerful Cholerics can hardly bear to evaluate their weaknesses. One of their greatest faults is their feeling they don't have any. Whatever your personal temperament pattern, think deeply and honestly about your weaknesses, and put down three that most need improvement.

———————————————————————————————

———————————————————————————————

———————————————————————————————

If you are really anxious to have a more pleasing personality, be willing to ask others for help.

Seek Other Opinions

Dare to ask others, "If I were going to work on one area of my personality, where do you think I should start?" Then do the hardest thing you'll ever have to do. Listen!

Don't tell them they are crazy. Don't be defensive and say, "Well you're worse." Whatever the person says, thank him and think it over. I've often had people give me unsolicited advice, slip me notes of constructive criticism in *Christian love*. While I never am excited about such suggestions, I have learned to think them over, pull out whatever truth there is, change what I can, and throw away the rest. There is usually some basic element of truth in the least positive of comments, and we grow when we accept what appears to be criticism with dignity and thankfulness.

Plan Your Steps for Personal Improvement

As you look at the three weaknesses you have chosen to work on, list what you can actually do to change these areas.

_____

_____

_____

Admitting you have them is the first step, but that is not enough.

What can you do to improve your human relationships? Popular Sanguines can bite their tongues until they learn to talk only half as much. Perfect Melancholies can stop each time they hear themselves being negative, and critical Powerful Cholerics can force themselves to listen to other opinions. Peaceful Phlegmatics can feign enthusiasm until it becomes natural. Change hurts, but without it we don't improve.

Ask Your Family for Help

There is nothing more appealing than a teachable spirit—one that asks for correction and accepts it with thanksgiving. As I have trained Marita to become a speaker, I have been encouraged by her willingness to learn from me, and her lack of defensiveness. I can make suggestions to her, and she will both thank me and put them into practice. A teachable spirit is a rare and beautiful attribute.

If you have this spirit, the step of asking for correction from your family will be easy; if not, you must pray for a right spirit within you before asking for help. Realize your family may not take you seriously at first. If you sense some skepticism from your family, it's probably because they don't believe you mean business. In the past, you may have put walls between you and others, and they don't dare to be honest with you.

If you are primarily *Popular Sanguine*, your family knows you have little resolve to stay with any correctional action that will take longer than today. You only want to hear the good and run from problems or criticism. Your family knows you don't really want to deal with your faults, and they may say, "You're just fine the way you are." If you're a typical Popular Sanguine you'll say, "Oh, good! Then I won't have to change." You will have to show real dedication to improvement before they will believe.

If you are *Perfect Melancholy*, you have manipulated the family with your moods for so long that they don't dare say a negative thing about you for fear of sending you into a depression. They'd rather live with your faults than risk telling you about them and having your face drop into its hurt and mournful expression. To get their cooperation, you will have to smile through adverse circumstances and sing in the rain.

If you are *Powerful Choleric*, you have probably controlled the family with an iron hand, and no one dares dispute you for fear of an outburst of anger. You will have to preface your questions with "I promise I won't get upset if you give me an honest opinion. I do want to change for the better." (Watch the look of shock and disbelief in their eyes!)

If you are *Peaceful Phlegmatic*, you have trouble deciding what weaknesses to work on, and may dump the whole list on the group and let *them* choose your faults. They may not get too serious about this project because your past ones have been postponed—somehow they died on the vine. You will need to show decisive determination to solicit cooperation.

Encourage Honest Opinion

When any of us takes the time to think about our interchanges with other people, we realize how little honest opinion we encourage. We build our boxes around us, people learn how near they dare come to our fence, and they develop a working relationship with us that may be utterly phony. Does your family have to humor you to keep peace? Do your coworkers know how close they can come before you get mad or moody? If people are having to handle you with kid gloves, maybe it's time you got honest with them and allowed them to be honest with you.

We have had so many couples tell us that when they sat down and went over the charts together, they had the first meaningful discussion they'd had in years. One woman said, "We've always been defensive with each other if we got too close to the problems, so we've both lived behind a facade. When we sat down and discussed the charts, it was the first time we'd verbalized our faults. It was as if the page was doing the talking, and so we didn't get mad at each other. The tool of the temperaments has changed our ability to communicate openly and honestly."

Some people build their walls so thick no one ever gets to know the real person inside. This is often their reason for doing so. ("If you really knew what I'm like inside, you wouldn't care for me.") Let's come out from behind our masks and dare to change. We don't need to be fenced in by our failures of the past; we need to step out into the field of future potential.

Anyone who loves knowledge wants to be told when he is wrong. It is stupid to hate being corrected.

Proverbs 12:1 GNB

CHAPTER 14

Opposites Attract

We have all heard that opposites attract. Fred and I are a perfect example of this statement, and in the years we have been working with the temperaments, we have seldom found people of the same personality pattern married to each other. When we look at the strengths of the individuals, it is a great asset to have the opposites united together. Since Popular Sanguines are lighthearted, they lift Perfect Melancholy. Since Perfect Melancholies are organized, they get Popular Sanguine pulled together. When we can look at our marriages and understand that one partner's strengths fill in the other's weaknesses, we can be grateful for our differences and stop trying to change the other person.

Popular Sanguine/Perfect Melancholy Relations

Before marriage we tend to see each other's good points. The few weaknesses that surface we know will disappear when this individual has the opportunity to live with someone as inspiring as we are. As Fred and I learned, this automatic transformation doesn't often take place.

When we first met, Fred was attracted to my Popular Sanguine personality. Since he did not like the small talk of social occasions, he felt if he married me I would do all the conversing for him—and I did! I could see in Fred the Perfect Melancholy depth and stability. I knew he could straighten out my life and get me organized—and he did!

We were attracted to the opposite strengths in each other and, although we didn't know this at the time, we were seeking to fill the missing pieces in our own personalities. Since we were two perfect people heading into what automatically would have to be a perfect marriage, we never considered the possibility of any problems; however, that hopeful thinking proved to be unrealistic.

Let's examine just one area in which we had an immediate conflict: the scheduling of our time. Before we were married, I managed to teach five different high-school courses each day, and direct all the drama activities without Fred's being on the scene at all. I felt I was organized, but the minute we got to Bermuda on our honeymoon, Fred began to chart out our time so we wouldn't waste our vacation on relaxation. He decided visiting old forts would be productive and after reading several brochures on the island's history, he laid out our procedures.

To cover the route efficiently, he rented us motorbikes. While he read over the instructions that came with the bikes, I started mine up, without knowing how to stop, and crashed into a stone wall that rose up as an instant barricade before me. The owner came screaming over, as he saw me in a heap and the front wheel of his bike overlapping the back one. Fred was humiliated to be seen with someone so dumb as to plunge off without a plan. He gave me a lecture that started with a phrase I later came to hate: "Everyone knows that . . . " After he made me feel stupid for my impulsive trip into the wall, he paid for the damages, and helped me mount a new bike, on which I had to sit still, while he reviewed the parts of a bike in terms simple enough for a first-grader to understand.

In the one incident I learned:

> Fred was smart—I was dumb
> Fred was strong—I was weak
> Fred was right—I was wrong

I didn't like any of these conclusions, but I lived with constant reminders of their validity for fifteen years, until we learned about the temperaments. Then each found that just because the other one is different doesn't make him *wrong*.

Misery Wants Company

On our way back from Bermuda on the *Ocean Monarch*, Fred got seasick before we left the harbor. He took to his bed and moaned "I wish

I were dead." I'd always disliked ailing people, and so I fled the whole sick scene. Neither of us knew anything about the personalities then. Fred was crushed because I didn't stay in the cabin, put cool cloths on his forehead, and commiserate with him. Perfect Melancholies love sympathy, are willing to sit with the sick themselves, and assume any decent person would attend the ailing.

I was disturbed that Fred was ruining my good time on the *Love Boat*, and after a few cheering words (to ease my conscience), I took off in pursuit of pleasure. Fred didn't realize that Popular Sanguines hate sickness, avoid anything unpleasant, and aim for action and fun.

Schedule? What Schedule?

A week after we returned from our honeymoon, we went to a movie, and as we came out I suggested, "Why don't we go to Howard Johnson's for an ice-cream cone?" I thought I had come up with a great idea, but Fred countered, "It's not on my schedule."

"What schedule?"

"I make out a schedule every morning at seven o'clock. If you want an ice-cream cone at eleven at night, you have to tell me at seven in the morning, so I can put it on my schedule."

"I didn't know at seven this morning that I'd want an ice-cream cone at eleven tonight."

We went straight home, and I knew this marriage was never going to be much fun.

Right from the start we had trouble with the toothpaste. Fred felt it essential to roll up the tube neatly from the bottom. I just grabbed it and squeezed. He kept straightening out my bumps and cleaning off the cap, and I didn't even notice what he was doing. One of the basic conflicts of Popular Sanguine and Perfect Melancholy married to each other is that Popular Sanguine doesn't know she is doing something wrong, and the quiet Perfect Melancholy doesn't want to state the problem clearly. He just quietly repairs the damages, assuming Popular Sanguine will sooner or later learn from observation. But Popular Sanguine doesn't get the hint, and so surely doesn't pick up the solution. By the time Perfect Melancholy feels he must make an issue of it, his emotions are so tense it turns into a major altercation. By understanding the personalities these problems can be avoided. Perfect Melancholy decides whether it's an important issue or not, and then speaks up before he gets upset. Popular Sanguine tries to do what's right and Perfect Melancholy learns to overlook the mistakes.

Fred solved our toothpaste problem by buying me my own tube and letting me squeeze it any old way.

Opposites *do* attract, and when we focus on the strengths, we fit fine, but when we don't understand our personalities, we tend to focus on the weaknesses and feel "someone different from me" must be wrong.

One couple I counseled had the typical Popular Sanguine/Perfect Melancholy problem. Chuck was a life-of-the-party type salesman, who always had something funny to say. Miriam, a Perfect Melancholy, told me how she was attracted to Chuck instantly because he had such confidence in himself, while she was insecure, socially ill at ease, and often withdrew from crowds. She described Chuck as outgoing, handsome, charming, talkative, and witty; these were all qualities she lacked and felt he would supply.

By the time Miriam came to me she was deeply depressed. She had wanted a perfect marriage, but Chuck didn't do things right. He was often late for dinner, which she always had ready on time, and she took this as a personal insult. What was worse, when he did arrive, he didn't even sense he was late. She wouldn't believe he was not a clock-watcher, as she was, so she felt he was late on purpose. She did not discuss the problem with him because she did not want to cause friction.

She noticed how disorganized he was, and how often he lost his keys. She bought a keyboard with hooks on it, and put it by the front door. She waited for him to notice it, and when he didn't, she sulked and he didn't know why. When she finally told him she was upset because he didn't see the key hooks she'd bought for him, he told her she was ridiculous. She sulked again.

After attending a few parties with Chuck, she realized how repetitious he was with his jokes. She had never liked levity, and she surely didn't like to hear the same corny tale over and over. One night he told a story that wasn't completely true, and she was shocked to realize her husband was a liar. She mentioned to him that he hadn't exactly told the truth, and he replied, "What difference does it make? They laughed, didn't they?"

When I talked to Chuck, he told *his* side. He was a delightful, charming man, and I could see why she fell for him. They were as mismatched as most couples, but he felt everything would be all right if she'd just loosen up.

"Miriam is a sweet, soft, shy girl, and I love that part of her—but she's been depressed half the time since we got married. She used to think I was funny—as everyone does—but now she calls me a liar and wants all my stories to be the plain facts.

"She's a great housekeeper; in fact she's close to fanatical. If I set my cup down, she whisks it off to the kitchen. We've got new living room furniture, and she has it all covered with sheets so it won't fade. I feel like I'm sitting around in a morgue. It's spooky.

"If I come home ten minutes late, she's depressed. She can't seem to understand I'm a salesman, and I have to hang in there until they sign. It's like I've married a mother, and I'm the bad little boy."

What are we going to do with Chuck and Miriam? Many problems are self-healing, once the participants can back up and look somewhat objectively at themselves. I gave these two a set of Personality Plus tapes and told them I wouldn't see them again until they had listened to them together. Miriam called a week later, and she sounded like a new person. "May I come over? We've been listening to the tapes."

This is what she told me:

I feel so stupid that I couldn't figure out our problems by myself. Listening to the tapes together was eye opening, as we both heard about ourselves. Chuck began to realize I wasn't trying to be his mother; I'm just a Perfect Melancholy who wants everything perfect. We began to talk openly for the first time, and I realized I had never told him how I felt. I'd just wanted him to read my mind, and when he didn't, I got depressed. We began to go over our differences. I had previously planned dinner for six o'clock, which I felt was the normal hour. He never got home before six-thirty—and I'd be upset. I've moved the time to seven o'clock, and we even have a few minutes to relax before dinner. I've learned there's no big prize for sitting down on schedule.

Chuck uses the key hooks now that he knows they're up. I regret the time I spent waiting for him to notice my good deed. As I listened to the tapes on Popular Sanguines telling stories, and I realized they all are more interested in response than accuracy, I realized he wasn't lying, and no one but me seemed to care. What I liked about him was how he could entertain everyone, and I've concluded he can tell it any way he wants. I won't correct him short of his making an inflammatory statement that would start World War III.

After our listening to the tapes, Chuck asked if we could possibly take the sheets off the furniture because it felt like a funeral home in there. Before, I would have been very hurt that he was criticizing my housework, but I even smiled and helped him pull them off. If the chairs fade ten years from now, we'll get new ones.

Thank you for making us listen to the tapes. It's shown me how serious and stuffy I've become, and how little fun I was for Chuck to be with. We can now discuss our differences and laugh about them.

It is amazing how other people improve when we understand their personalities and don't try to make them become like us. What a blessing it is when we can learn to accept the slightly irregular *just as they are*.

You have probably all heard case histories similar to this. Your own life may be far more colorful than this one, and you may be saying to yourself, *If she thinks this couple has problems, she should hear* my *story!* Everyone's own story is the worst, because it's personal and omnipresent, but understanding the personalities of individuals can help solve situations before they get out of hand.

Powerful Choleric/Peaceful Phlegmatic Relations

Peaceful Phlegmatics don't like to be pushed, and yet when they are left on their own, they don't get around to doing what they promised to do. Dotty, a Powerful Choleric friend of mine who is trying to keep from running everything in the home, gave her Peaceful Phlegmatic husband, Lewis, a major decision to make. In discussing vacation plans, he chose a certain resort on the coast. Lewis was to make the reservations. Each time Dotty asked if he had made them yet, he told her he would do it when he was ready, and she should stop nagging him. On the day they were leaving, Dotty summoned up a smile of hope and asked sweetly, "I assume you did make the reservations." His low-key comment was, "They always have cancellations." She was furious, and they drove in silence to San Diego.

When they asked the desk clerk for a reservation, he laughed at them. "You expect to walk into a beach resort in August and pick up a room? You must be kidding. There's not a space in town."

"That was insult enough," Dotty told me, "but then Lewis turned to me and said, 'You should have reminded me to call.' I lost my mind on that, burst into tears, and ran out to the car where I hit my fists on the fenders. I vowed I'd never count on him for anything again."

They finally found one room in an old motel next to an all-night diner. Lewis went promptly to sleep on the lumpy mattress, while Dotty lay awake livid all night.

In the morning Lewis said, "This may not be a luxury motel, but think of the money we saved."

Unfortunately, this scenario is typical of the merry-go-round the Powerful Choleric wife and Peaceful Phlegmatic husband are on. He doesn't want to be pushed around and tells her so. She holds back, and then tries not to check on him. He neglects his responsibilities, and the ax falls. She gets upset and knows she can't trust him. She takes back control, and he tells everyone she picks on him. She comes across as the heavy, and he looks like the typical henpecked husband.

Repairing the Damage

To repair these types of problems, the couples first have to understand their conflicting temperaments, and then pledge together to work from the extremes toward the center. No matter which sex they are, Popular Sanguines have to get their lives pulled together, while Perfect Melancholies realize how hard this is for them to do. Perfect Melancholy has to lower his standards and not get depressed if he finds he's married to an imperfect person.

Powerful Choleric has to let Peaceful Phlegmatic make decisions and be responsible, and Peaceful Phlegmatic had best follow through, so the Powerful Choleric won't take back the reins. Peaceful Phlegmatic should force himself to plan interesting activities, and Powerful Choleric should take time from work to enjoy them.

All these acts take effort but the alternative is two married people living two separate lives, until the day one of them decides to leave.

There is hope! Fred and I made the supreme effort to turn our marriage around. I had to learn to get organized, and he had to learn to have fun, but we cared enough to do it and we did. Many who have attended our seminars have written to say how much the knowledge of the personalities has helped them.

> *Personality merges in marriage and "you only reach your new identity when you are merged with another person. . . . Love is the outpouring of one personality in fellowship with another personality."*

> Oswald Chambers

CHAPTER **15**

We Can Recognize Differences in Others

Once we have an understanding of ourselves through the study of the four personalities, we can open up a whole new world of positive human relationships. We can take the principles we've learned and apply them in a practical direction.

We can know:

Popular Sanguines are best:
- in dealing with people enthusiastically
- in expressing thoughts with excitement
- in up-front positions of attention

Perfect Melancholies are best:
- in attending to details and in deep thinking
- in keeping records, charts, and graphs
- in analyzing problems too difficult for others

Powerful Cholerics are best:
- in jobs that require quick decisions
- in spots that need instant action and accomplishments
- in areas that demand strong control and authority

Peaceful Phlegmatics are best:
- in positions of mediation and unity
- in storms that need a calming hand
- in routines that might seem dull to others

As we go through the Personality Principles, begin to plan your use of this knowledge to improve your ability to get along with others. Each temperament has its own style of body language, of speaking, and of social behavior. As we begin to understand the different personalities and start to observe people, we will find that we can often recognize a person's personality pattern as he enters a room. We should never use this knowledge to judge or label anyone, but just to help us in our relationships with others and in anticipating reactions.

Popular Sanguine

Popular Sanguine comes into a party with his mouth open, looking for an audience. As he talks noisily to draw attention to his entrance, his hands are always moving. If Popular Sanguine has to sit, he will wiggle, tap his foot, drum with his fingers—anything rather than sit still.

He cannot just rest quietly and relax. He is always looking for his next audience and will leave you in the middle of your best story to run off to a new friend who has just entered. He won't even realize he was rude for he was not listening and did not notice that you were talking. During a party, Popular Sanguine will flit from group to group, and the noise level will pick up wherever he is. The Popular Sanguine woman will enter with hugs, kisses, shrieks, and laughter, and as she talks, she will have her audience held tightly in her hands, in order to keep them from getting away before the punch line. When you see a loud, talkative, exuberant person bounce into the room, you will probably be observing a Popular Sanguine.

Popular Sanguine talks in colorful extremes without any necessary relationship to the truth. Popular Sanguine feels that if she has heard a dull story that she must pass on, it is only logical that she should dress it up a bit, so you will hear the tale in better form than she received it.

Whatever Popular Sanguine says, it will be exaggerated and exuberant, and you won't have any trouble hearing it. Once you spot Popular Sanguine, you can make a quick decision. If you want to be entertained, stay. If you want to talk yourself, quickly flee to another room and find a sedentary Peaceful Phlegmatic who will listen.

Powerful Choleric

Powerful Choleric, like Popular Sanguine, finds it hard to relax, and he tends to sit on the edge of his chair, waiting for some action. Small talk is usually a waste of time for Powerful Choleric, and if the conversation cannot be on business or something he can straighten out, he would rather not talk at all. When Powerful Choleric sees something he wants, he tends to reach for it, instead of asking, and he may, in the process, knock over the centerpiece.

Powerful Choleric knows everything about every subject and will be glad to tell you more than you need to know about anything. He speaks in absolutes and tends to look at others as if they were prize dummies. It is better not to disagree with him in a social situation for he loves to argue and he will prove you wrong even if you are right. You will find it difficult to escape from his proof, and he may follow you to the car, expounding his logic until you dutifully agree that black is white. Powerful Choleric can be heard to say things such as:

"I *told* you so."
"Watch out, you dummy!"
"Absolutely not."
"Obviously."
"Only an idiot would say such a thing."
"What *is* the matter with you?"
"Haven't you ever learned *anything*?"
"If you only had half a wit about you, you could see I'm right."

Once you learn to recognize a Powerful Choleric, you will know how to deal with one in a social situation. Ask him difficult questions and be openly impressed with his answers. Nod intelligently at his major truths of life, and he will remember you as a brilliant conversationalist.

Perfect Melancholy

In contrast to the loud, strong entrance of Popular Sanguine and Powerful Choleric, Perfect Melancholy will enter quietly and unobtrusively. The man is hopeful that no one will notice him, and the Perfect Melancholy woman is sure that she wore the wrong thing. The Perfect Melancholy man does not like parties anyway, and he is sorry he even came. Perfect Melancholy tends to stand around the fringes of the group with his hands in his pockets, and he will not take a chair unless he is specifically asked to sit down. He never wants to offend anyone, and he never wants to give the hostess the opportunity of saying anything critical of him later. He often takes some flip statement made by some unthinking Popular Sanguine deeply to heart, and he may go into a mild depression and refuse to talk for the rest of the evening. At the first opportunity, he will drag his wife out the front door and get back to the security of his own home, wondering why he ever left it in the first place.

Perfect Melancholy finds it very difficult to accept compliments and usually replies with such comments as:

"You like this old thing?"
"I have always hated my hair."
"Oh, you're just saying that. It's really dreadful."
"I'm really no good at this at all."

Since Perfect Melancholy often has a negative self-image, he tends to say:

"There's not much hope for this whole project."
"With my luck, it will fall apart."
"I could never be the president."
"I knew the whole thing was wrong from the beginning."
"I'll probably ruin the entire meal."
"I don't think they really want me on the committee."
"I knew I would wear the wrong thing."
"I never know what to say."
"I wish I'd stayed home."

Once you recognize a Perfect Melancholy, you know that you can have a deep and meaningful conversation and that he will appreciate a serious and sincere approach. Perfect Melancholy does not enjoy loud comments, and he will not like it if you draw attention to him. He would rather have one intelligent conversation in an evening than to flit from person to person as Popular Sanguine does.

Peaceful Phlegmatic

Peaceful Phlegmatic comes in slowly, with a half-smile, amused that so many people came to such an unimportant gathering. He gives a casual look at the group and hopes he will be able to stay awake. Since he believes that one should never stand when one can sit, and never sit when one can lie down, he heads dutifully for the softest chair he can find. He collapses into the cushions and almost folds up like a lawn chair before your very eyes. He takes the evening easily and relaxes, yawns a lot, and may even doze off. If Peaceful Phlegmatic gets inadvertently involved in the conversation of the evening, he will usually throw in a few witty comments timed properly. These bits of dry humor often go unnoticed for they are inserted in such an unobtrusive manner, and one really has to be paying attention to pick up their subtle value.

Since Peaceful Phlegmatic would rather relax than exert any noticeable energy, and since he does not have any burning crusade to promote, he tends to talk in somewhat indifferent clichés.

"What does it matter?"

"Well, that's the way the ball bounces."

"Now, let's not get all excited over nothing."

"It's always been that way, and why should we start changing things now?"

"Why bother?"

"It just sounds too much like work."

Peaceful Phlegmatics tend to band together at parties and sit quietly. There is a certain comfort in knowing that they don't expect anything of each other, and that they can mutually bask in each other's acceptance of the status quo. If you are looking for an audience or for someone who won't argue with you, try a Peaceful Phlegmatic. You'll like him.

The next time you are at a gathering, look around and see the Popular Sanguine lady grabbing onto every available male and bubbling over with adorable stories. Observe the Powerful Choleric man firmly telling the other men how to get their businesses straightened out, so that they can be successful like him. Watch the Perfect Melancholy lady, sitting properly and insecurely, while the men are attracted by her soft and gentle spirit (and she hopes that they aren't saying nice things just to make her happy). Then locate Peaceful Phlegmatic relaxed by the TV in the family room, hoping that no one will find him. Don't be surprised if his eyes are half-shut and he is saying to himself, *This party isn't so bad after all.*

The knowledge of the personalities can help each one of us to function better in social situations, to converse in a manner that will be appropriate and pleasing to the others present, and to understand the positives and the negatives of other people. From here on, you will have more fun as you learn to spot the talker, the doer, the thinker, and the watcher. Isn't it wonderful that we were not all made alike?

Teach a wise man, and he will be the wiser; teach a good man, and he will learn more.

Proverbs 9:9 TLB

CHAPTER **16**

How to Get Along with Others

Now that we have analyzed our own strengths and weaknesses and have begun a program to work sincerely and prayerfully to improve, how can we use this knowledge to help us get along with others?

One day young Fred was complaining to me about Marita. In his Perfect Melancholy way, he told me she was too noisy, never serious, and not neat. "I have to pick up after her all the time, and I'm sick of it." I turned to him and said, "Do you know why God gave you Marita for a sister? He wanted to give you years of practice in living with a Popular Sanguine, because He knows you'll marry a girl just like Marita."

"I will never marry anyone like Marita," he stated clearly, and left the room.

Several days later when my Popular Sanguine mind had totally forgotten the conversation, he came into the kitchen and said, "You're right."

I had no idea about what, but I was thrilled I was at least right.

"You're right I'll probably marry someone like Marita. I've been sitting in school all week, watching the girls I like, and they're all just like Marita. I guess I'd better learn to get along with her."

I didn't mention the incident to Marita, and a week later she asked, "Is Fred after something?"

"Why?"

"He's been so nice to me and he even helped me carry some things in from the car."

171

I explained, "He's agreed with me that he'll probably marry a Popular Sanguine, and he's practicing up on you."

When we begin to understand the differences in our basic temperaments, it takes the pressure off our human relationships. We can look at each other's differences in a positive way and not try to make everyone to be like us.

The Popular Sanguine Personality

Recognize Their Difficulty in Accomplishing Tasks

Much as we wish every Popular Sanguine would shape up, this thought is unlikely, so we might as well be realistic. Popular Sanguines love new ideas and projects, but they are very poor on follow-through. This weakness is especially difficult for Perfect Melancholies to understand, because they have such a need to finish what they start and think every intelligent person would feel the same. Little Popular Sanguine children need constant supervision to see that they do what they are assigned. They are easily distracted, but they really mean well, so don't give up. Many mothers feel it's easier to do things themselves, but that attitude only encourages Popular Sanguines' weaknesses, and they soon learn if they do poorly they won't be asked again.

Since Popular Sanguine adults are just bigger children, the same principle applies. If you are supervising Popular Sanguines, you have to make the instructions clear, even *urgent* would help, and then follow through, until you can trust them to finish a project. It is always best to employ Popular Sanguines in areas where they shine, and keep them from detailed duties that demand split-second timing.

Realize They Talk without Thinking First

Perfect Melancholies can't understand that anyone would open their mouths without knowing what they were going to say. Popular Sanguines open their mouths to find out what they are saying. They are not trying to be thoughtless, it just happens. One Popular Sanguine told me, "My husband says my mind is like a gumball machine—all bright colored thoughts rolling around in no particular order and when you press a button they come pouring out by the handful."

Realize They Like Variety and Flexibility

Popular Sanguines always want something new going on, and they do best when an aura of fun is acceptable. Putting them in routine, dull jobs will not maximize their abilities. A Popular Sanguine woman wants lots of clothes, money, parties, and friends, and doesn't want to settle down to the prosaic side of life. Popular Sanguine men tend to get enthused over a new job and do well until the uniqueness wears off. If you want a steady, dependable, conservative husband, you'd better not take a chance on a Popular Sanguine. If you want excitement, variety, and no dull moments, the Popular Sanguine is your man.

Help Them to Keep from Accepting More Than They Can Do

Popular Sanguines frequently get overcommitted, because they become enthused at every new idea or project and agree to join up (or even be president). They also have difficulty in saying *no* to anyone. Popular Sanguines mean well, but they flee when they are overwhelmed. Help them to analyze their available time and take on only what they can handle. Mates of Popular Sanguines tend to wait until the day the nervous breakdown arrives, and then make them drop out of everything forever. Try to deal with this problem early and rationally, knowing Popular Sanguines need outside activities but can't say *no* to anyone. Be impressed that they were asked; compliment their charisma; and help them decline a few outstanding opportunities to be center stage, but don't cut off *all* their outside activities.

Don't Expect Them to Remember Appointments or Be on Time

Although I have already pleaded with Popular Sanguines to get their lives pulled together and be on time, don't you count on it. Even when they plan to be early something always happens. Even if they leave on time, they have to go back for what they forgot.

It is a miracle Marita and Fred ever got straight teeth with the number of orthodontist appointments I never got them to. Luckily, the doctor was closeted in some inner sanctum, protected by a bevy of young girls in short skirts, so I never had to face him. I'm sure if you asked him about *me*, he would say I must be some poor confused lady with twelve children, a low IQ, and no calendar.

Try as they may, Popular Sanguines can't quite make it all click at once.

Praise Them for Everything They Accomplish

Because it is so difficult for Popular Sanguines to get to the far end of any project, they need constant praise to keep them going. Other temperaments who don't need such frequent bolstering don't understand that compliments are food for Popular Sanguines. They can't live without them.

When Fred and I were first married and I would clean all the crumbs out of the knife drawer, I would ask for praise. "Fred, I cleaned the knife drawer."

"It's about time. It sure needed attention."

With that kind of response, I gave up on cleaning drawers. As Fred learned how to handle me by understanding my temperament, he realized how important encouragement is to me. Now when I clean the knife drawer and let him know, he drops everything and runs right over. "Oh, what a lovely knife drawer!" With that I may some day clean another.

With Popular Sanguine children, it is especially important to acknowledge what they have accomplished, rather than pointing out how poorly they did it. Compliment a few trivia today, and they may do a few more tomorrow.

Remember They Are Circumstantial People

More than any other temperament, Popular Sanguines are controlled by their circumstances. Their emotions go up and down according to what is happening around them. When you realize how quickly their emotions change, you won't overreact to their hysteria. It's unfortunate for Popular Sanguines that they cry "Wolf!" too often. One lady told me she leaned over a gas burner and her sleeve caught on fire. She screamed to her husband in the other room, "Help! Help! I'm on fire!" and he called back, "You sure are, honey. You're hot stuff!"

Bring Them Presents; They Like New Toys

Oh, how Popular Sanguine likes to get gifts. It doesn't matter how magnificent the gift might be, if you bring *any* present he will get excited. Fred has learned how much I love surprises, and if he buys a loaf of bread on his way home, he calls me in and presents it to me as a gift. I open the bag and am truly grateful he had noticed I was low on bread, when I was oblivious. One Easter he brought me home a dozen chartreuse coat hangers he'd found on sale. I was excited, because we have a coat hanger thief, and I can never find a spare hanger. Now that I have chartreuse ones, I can patrol other closets and easily spot the stolen hangers.

Since Popular Sanguines stay wide-eyed and childlike forever, they are always looking for a new toy to brighten up their day.

Accept That They Make Fun Out of What Would Be Embarrassing to Others

Popular Sanguines love to tell stories of their mistakes so listen and don't try to tell them how they could have avoided the problem. One lady told me she was standing at a street corner at lunch time. There was a traffic jam that had all cars stopped, and the police were keeping all pedestrians out of the streets. Being part Powerful Choleric and not wanting to waste time, she decided to clean out her handbag while waiting. She dumped out the contents of her bag on the hood of a car she perceived to be parked at the curb. As she was sorting through the pile, the traffic jam broke, the police signaled the cars to move and the car she was using as a table lunged off into the intersection scattering her belongings to the winds. She went screaming after her assorted possessions and soon all the pedestrians were dodging cars and picking up her papers, bottles, combs, lipsticks, and money. She got all the important things back, she hopes, and she could hardly wait to tell me this story that would have humiliated a Perfect Melancholy personality.

Realize They Mean Well

Perhaps the most important advice on getting along with Popular Sanguines is to realize that they do mean well. So many Perfect Melancholies have told me what a help it is to them to know Popular Sanguine isn't out to get them. Popular Sanguines want so much to be popular and well liked that they try to be pleasing, and they don't *mean* to give anyone any trouble. When you accept this fact, you will have far fewer conflicts with the Popular Sanguines.

Appreciate their sense of fun.

The Perfect Melancholy Personality

Know That They Are Very Sensitive and Get Hurt Easily

One of the greatest benefits of learning about the personalities is the relief you feel when you can understand why another person reacts as he does. For Popular Sanguines and Powerful Cholerics, who tend to say what's on their minds without thinking, it is so important to know that Perfect Melancholies are very sensitive and get hurt easily.

This same trait of sensitivity is a positive that gives Perfect Melancholies their rich, deep, emotional natures, but carried to an extreme, these feelings cause them to be hurt easily. As soon as you know a person is of a Perfect Melancholy temperament, watch your words and your volume and you will avoid having a dejected person on your hands.

If you see the black cloud come down over the head, apologize sincerely, and explain that you have a tendency to speak too quickly without thinking.

Realize They Are Programmed with a Pessimistic Attitude

Until you understand Perfect Melancholies, you don't realize that they come prepackaged with a pessimistic view of life. This trait is positive, because they are able to look ahead and see the problems other temperaments don't notice, but carried to an extreme they never seem to have a happy moment.

Learn to Deal With Depression

For those of you living with a Perfect Melancholy who gets deeply depressed, I would again suggest you read my book *Blow Away the Black Clouds*. This is a layman's book on the symptoms of depression, with suggestions for overcoming them. The chapter "How to Live With a Depressed Person" will be especially helpful.

Here are a few basics:

1. Watch for Signs of Depression:
   Loss of interest in life
   Feelings of pessimism and hopelessness
   Withdrawal from others
   Overeating or undereating
   Insomnia or inability to stay awake
   Talk of suicide
2. Realize They Need Help. If your concern and counsel are rejected, try to get the affected person to talk with someone whom he respects on the subject of his feelings.
3. Don't Try to Jolly Them Up. Before I understood depression, I would treat Fred's dips by saying cheerfully, "Come on and be happy like me." I soon learned my jollity only sank him deeper into the pit he was already in. We have to get down in the hole with them, tell them we understand how they feel (and don't blame them), and then walk up step-by-step together.
4. Encourage Them to Express Their Feelings. Popular Sanguines and Powerful Cholerics treat depression as something that can be turned off with a switch. Their answer is "Cheer up and snap out of it." If the person doesn't respond instantly, they tend to take off and leave him with his problems. The depressed person needs time to pour out his feelings, to examine the cause with someone, and to analyze possible solutions.
5. Never Tell Them Their Problems Are Stupid. The depressed person feels that his problems, while real, may also be stupid. He gets mad at himself for being moody, and he knows everyone will think his concerns are ridiculous. Because of these feelings,

he doesn't tell anyone what's bothering him. If you plead with him, he will finally share. Imagine what happens to his psyche when he dares to share and you state, "Why that's the stupidest thing I ever heard of!"

Compliment Them Sincerely and Lovingly

Because Perfect Melancholies are insecure in the love of others, they look with question on the compliments they receive. While Popular Sanguine is so eager for good words that he will take an insult and turn it into a compliment, Perfect Melancholy often takes a compliment and turns it into an insult! Another reason for their doubt of a casual, uplifting word is they are analytical of everything and suspicious of people, especially happy people. They feel there must be an ulterior motive behind a compliment, and yet they really want to be appreciated. This conflict makes it difficult for anyone to give a positive word to a Perfect Melancholy and have it received as it was intended. Knowing this should help you to give sincere, quiet, and loving compliments and to not be upset if the response is "What did you really mean by that?"

Accept That They Like It Quiet Sometimes

Before I married Fred I didn't know it was possible to be both quiet and happy. I thought to be alone ten minutes a day was equal to being unpopular. I'd studied radio announcing, and you could be *fired* if there were five seconds of dead air. I viewed life in the same vein. Someone had to be talking at all times, and dead air equaled boredom. Imagine my amazement when, after I'd talked straight through the honeymoon, Fred announced, "I really enjoy life best when it's quiet."

Enjoy Quiet?

Such a revolutionary thought. If you are a Popular Sanguine, you may not know Perfect Melancholies *really* like moments of dead air. They enjoy staring into space, inhaling a fresh breeze, meditating in the moonlight. If you can understand this principle, you will be appreciated by the sensitive Perfect Melancholy.

Try to Keep a Reasonable Schedule

The most important part of life to any Perfect Melancholy is his schedule. He needs to know where he is going, when, and why. A day without direction is a cause for insurrection. Once you accept this fact, you can improve your relationship with your Perfect Melancholies by working to get your life on some kind of a schedule. Don't try to pull Perfect Melancholy into your haphazard style of life. He's right. We should all know where we're going.

Realize That Neatness Is a Necessity

The fastest way to put a Perfect Melancholy into a depression is to scatter things all over the house and never know where anything is. Even if you are Popular Sanguine, try to establish some sense of order, pick up things instead of stepping over them, put things back after you use them.

Perfect Melancholies often carry their desire for perfection to extremes such as the man who said to his Popular Sanguine bride, "If you don't learn to sleep neater, I'll get a separate bed."

Help Them Not to Become Slaves to the Family (a special note for men with Perfect Melancholy wives!)

Because Perfect Melancholies are perfectionists, it is difficult for them to accept work not up to their standards. Consequently, Perfect Melancholy mothers tend to do all the work and become slaves to the family. Once the children grasp their mother's devotion to dusting, they will perform poorly enough to prod her into saying, "I don't ever want you to do another thing around this house." They will smile with satisfaction and go out to play forever. While the children will be relieved, they will learn little about housekeeping and have a distorted view of responsibilities in life. Encourage your wife to train the children to be helpers and to lower *her* standards even with *their* abilities.

Be grateful that you have a deeply sensitive and emotional partner.

The Powerful Choleric Personality

Recognize They Are Born Leaders

The first thing to understand in dealing with Powerful Cholerics is that they are born leaders, and their nature nudges them into control positions. They are not Peaceful Phlegmatics who one day made a major decision to take over the world. They are not Perfect Melancholies who designed plans and determined to put them into aggressive action. They are not Popular Sanguines who finally got down to business. They are people who were born with a desire to direct and a love for leadership. A Powerful Choleric child observed his Powerful Choleric father yell at his Peaceful Phlegmatic mother. Even though he didn't know the personality differences, he comforted his weeping mother by stating, "When he yells at you, you just yell right back!" Once you understand their nature, full of positive traits, sometimes carried to extremes, you won't be surprised or hurt when they take charge.

Because Powerful Cholerics are so strong, those dealing with them have to counter with similar strength. They don't mean to force their own way, they just quickly see the logical answer to situations and assume you want what's "right." Once you understand their thinking pattern you can stand firm, and they will respect you for this position. When you allow Powerful Choleric to push you around, he will continue to do so.

Insist on Two-Way Communication

The controlling nature of Powerful Choleric makes it difficult for the partner to assert any will in household activities or plans. Because of this problem, the husband or wife of Powerful Choleric must insist on some two-way communication. *Insist* is a strong word, but it is a needed one in conversing with Powerful Choleric, for he will scoff at your need to discuss matters and just give you answers.

Sometimes I've suggested to women with Powerful Choleric husbands that they hear him out, thank him for his message, and ask for three-minute rebuttal time. He will usually pay attention if you are clear and concise, firm yet friendly.

Know They Don't Mean to Hurt

Because Powerful Cholerics spit out what they think instantly, without concern for someone else's feelings, they frequently hurt people. If we realize Powerful Choleric doesn't mean to hurt, that he just speaks straight out, we will more easily accept his quick comments and not be upset.

When a Powerful Choleric came up to me and said, "I like your dress, and I've liked it every time you've worn it," I did not go home and burn the dress. She wasn't trying to hurt me; she just said what was going through her mind in the order it passed through.

Don't Push Your Luck

If your relationship with Powerful Choleric is going smoothly, don't look for trouble or do anything that might set off a negative reaction. Children learn early in life not to push a Powerful Choleric parent or take chances.

One day I was talking on the phone with my Popular Sanguine grandson Jonathan when I heard a disturbance in the background.

"What's happening Jonathan?" I asked.

"My mother is yelling at Bryan."

"Is she very upset?"

"Not with me. It's Bryan."

"How are the rest of you doing?"

Then came the wise reply of this ten-year-old.

"We're all hanging right there on the line, and I'm not about to push it to see what will happen."

Try to Divide Areas of Responsibility

In order to keep out of trouble (and yet not give up *your* personality), you must get Powerful Choleric to discuss what family responsibilities he wishes, and what ones you are to control. Fred and I disagreed on such a simple thing as where to hang the kitchen tools. I felt I was in charge of the kitchen, and I wanted them where they looked pretty. Fred wanted them where they were practical. As we discussed this minor problem, I realized that he makes breakfast for me every morning, and if I didn't let him put the spatula where he could reach it, he might quit turning eggs.

Now that I travel so much, we have had to change some of the areas of responsibility that we had formerly arranged. Fred now does all the marketing and keeps the cabinets and refrigerator stocked, so when I come home there will be food available. Powerful Cholerics usually want the most practical plan, and they are not afraid of work, but if the duties are not clear there will be a conflict.

Realize They Are Not Compassionate

Since Powerful Choleric deals in reality and practicality, he is not apt to have compassion for the sick or weak, love for the unlovely, or time for hospital visitations. Powerful Cholerics tend to look the other way when there are emotional needs to be filled. They aren't mean or cruel; they just don't have a heart for those hurting. While Powerful Choleric should aim to improve his feelings for people, you will deal better with him if you don't expect miracles.

One Powerful Choleric pastor told me he makes it clear to his people that if they get sick he will make one hospital visit. "After that you are on your own."

Know They Are Always Right

Right from early childhood Powerful Cholerics know they are right. Our Powerful Choleric grandchild Bryan was playing a game with Fred. Bryan was about three at the time and was not playing by the rules. Fred, being Perfect Melancholy, thought that even little children should play by the rules, and he pointed out "Bryan you are wrong."

Bryan countered instantly, "I am not wrong. I am wight."

Amazingly enough the Powerful Choleric individual is the most apt to make correct judgments instinctively. So if you are unsure of which way to turn, follow the powerful personality.

Be grateful you have a leader who's "always right"!

The Peaceful Phlegmatic Personality

Realize They Need Direct Motivation

It is extremely difficult for the Powerful Choleric parent to understand a Peaceful Phlegmatic child. Because Powerful Choleric is so motivated and sees everything in the steps to a goal, he cannot comprehend that a child can have a low-level motivation, and yet not be stupid. He equates intelligence with thinking like he does, and may dampen the spirits of a Peaceful Phlegmatic, turning him into a loser.

A famous surgeon told me about his "withdrawn, lazy son with no personality." As we discussed the problem, I could see how this man's overbearing, conceited nature would cause any child to withdraw and appear lazy. He said, "I try to motivate the boy. Every time I see him sitting down, I say, 'Get up, you bum, and get to work.'"

You can imagine how much this command inspires the son!

Peaceful Phlegmatics are the most enjoyable, easygoing people there are, but they need positive motivation. They need parents or mates who encourage them and help them set goals. When we understand the Peaceful Phlegmatic temperament, we know they need direct motivation, and whether it's with a child, a mate, or a coworker, we can uplift, encourage, and lead, instead of looking down, judging, and wiping out their incentive.

Help Them Set Goals and Make Rewards

When I was in grammar school, our teachers gave us gold stars when we did our work well. I loved to see those stars up there, and I worked hard to receive a row of these rewards.

As we grow up we still like some type of reinforcement, and Peaceful Phlegmatic positively needs help in setting goals and rewards to make the effort worthwhile. The Peaceful Phlegmatic child will work far better if he has a chart of duties to check off. The Peaceful Phlegmatic wife will be a better housekeeper if the family notices what she's done, and the Peaceful Phlegmatic husband may clean the garage if he's promised apple pie for dessert.

Peaceful Phlegmatics are able to set goals, but their nature keeps them from wanting to—if they can avoid thinking that far ahead. As you learn to live with Peaceful Phlegmatics, you will realize how much they will accomplish if you have first taken the time to help them set goals and have explained the value of attainment.

A light at the end of the tunnel makes the long, dark crawl worthwhile.

Don't Expect Enthusiasm

Popular Sanguines and Powerful Cholerics want others to respond with enthusiasm to whatever they mention, and when Peaceful Phlegmatics don't appear interested, the others get hurt or upset. Once we all understand that the Peaceful Phlegmatic nature is not excitable, we can more easily accept the fact that those with that temperament don't jump for joy over new ideas.

One of the greatest assets in learning about temperaments is the pressure it removes from our expectations of others. Peaceful Phlegmatic Joe started one morning by saying, "Oh, I can tell this is going to be another rotten day." Powerful Choleric Carolyn answered, "I think you should count on it then. I'm sure you won't be disappointed."

Realize That Putting Things Off Is Their Form of Quiet Control

Since Peaceful Phlegmatics usually feel overwhelmed by their Powerful Choleric mates, they use procrastination as their tool of defense.

Paul confessed to me that he was a procrastinator. "I wait until the last minute and then rush it through." His Powerful Choleric wife Jean quickly countered, "You're right about waiting until the last minute, but you've never rushed through anything in your life!" Right there before my eyes they discussed heatedly the basement full of lumber waiting to be made into walls, the pool cover that had never been taken out of the shipping carton, and the shrubs that had died in the garage without ever seeing the light of day. As Jean was approaching the rage level, Paul calmly taunted, "Don't nag or you'll never get any of it done."

Force Them to Make Decisions

Peaceful Phlegmatics are capable of making decisions, but they often take the path of least resistance by letting others choose what to do and where to do it. Since they tend to avoid anything that would lead to controversy, they prefer not to rock the boat. In a social relationship, this middle-of-the-road approach is inoffensive—in fact it's often welcome. In a living situation, however, it is important that Peaceful Phlegmatic make at least some of the decisions.

In dealing with little children, don't accept a steady diet of "I don't care," but force them into looking at both sides of an issue, and then making a decision, even if they *don't care*. Explain how important it will be later in life for them to be able to evaluate clearly and make decisions.

In a husband-wife situation, Peaceful Phlegmatic must be forced to at least enter into family discussions and help solve issues. If you are a strongly opinionated person, you must give Peaceful Phlegmatic areas to control and keep your hands off. Often the reason Peaceful Phlegmatics won't decide is that they know the other person will do it his way anyway. To foster decisiveness, you must give the other person the reins and then live with the consequences. To do this is very difficult for Powerful Choleric, because he can see what's going wrong instantly and will want to jump in and correct the situation. After he salvages the remains a few times, the mate will give up and withdraw from any family leadership.

Don't Heap All the Blame on Them

Because Peaceful Phlegmatics are so quiet and accept the status quo, they are easy targets for those bolder temperaments who want to dump their guilt on someone else. I've often observed situations where Powerful Choleric made a hasty decision, the results were disastrous, and he heaped the blame on the available Peaceful Phlegmatic. Check yourself in this area, and see if you make the fault fall on others.

One Peaceful Phlegmatic lady told me her husband made her choose which type of dog the family should have, and then every time the dog made a mistake the blame was placed on her.

Even though Peaceful Phlegmatics may accept what's put upon them, this tactic lowers their self-esteem, causes them to withdraw from relationships with you, and leads them away from any future responsibilities.

If you use the Peaceful Phlegmatic for a wastebasket today, you may have a basket case on your hands tomorrow.

Encourage Them to Accept Responsibilities

Popular Sanguines have to stay away from accepting too many presidencies because they overextend themselves, and Powerful Cholerics have to keep from running everything they get their hands on. Peaceful Phlegmatics, however, avoid being in charge of *anything*, even though they have administrative ability and get along well with everyone. Because of their gifts of conciliatory leadership, they should be encouraged to accept responsibilities. They make excellent executives, and yet they tend to turn down promotions because they have been made to feel inadequate by others. They don't want to be left "holding the bag."

Don't accept their first *no*, but continue to show them the confidence you have in their abilities to lead. What better chairman, president, or king could you have than one who is easy to get along with— one who doesn't make hasty decisions, and one who can effectively mediate personality problems?

Appreciate their even dispositions.

Want to get along with others? Nothing succeeds like kindness.

Kind words are like honey—enjoyable and healthful.

Proverbs 16:24 TLB

PART FIVE

Personality Power

A Source of Strength to Achieve Our Potential

CHAPTER 17

Personality Plus Power Produces Positive People!

In the opening of this book, we asked why many self-improvement courses don't seem to work; why the changes don't last. The first answer to this problem is that most programs do not take into account the differences in temperaments. They tend to be taught by Powerful Cholerics for Powerful Cholerics. Now that we understand the temperaments, we know how Powerful Cholerics love to lead, and we know how quickly they grasp new purposes and plans and charge forth to show themselves they can make the goal. They are instantly motivated to action as long as they can see some benefits for themselves.

The Powerful Choleric/Perfect Melancholy combination will have the ability to aim for the goal and to chart out specific steps of achievement, but what happens to the other temperaments when presented with the initial material?

Popular Sanguine gets enthused over the possibility of getting his life pulled together. He sees visions of grandeur and sincerely wants to improve, but he never seems to find the time to get started, and when he does, he's lost the materials.

Perfect Melancholy who leans in the Peaceful Phlegmatic direction will take notes and analyze all that's offered. He may study the concepts and evaluate the merits. He may pull out some practical part of the program, but to face a major overhaul will be depressing.

Peaceful Phlegmatic, if he sees a few easy steps that might be useful, may head in a positive direction, but chances are the whole scope of the seminar will be overwhelming and just "too much like work."

Freed from Guilt

As I have been teaching the temperaments over the years, I have seen so many people freed from guilt when they realized why they didn't react in the so-called normal way to motivational material. Popular Sanguine needs to get organized but not feel guilty that he can't file all of life away in manila folders. Perfect Melancholy needs to loosen up and be more personable but not feel guilty when he doesn't turn into Bob Hope overnight. Peaceful Phlegmatic should increase his motivation and get moving but not feel guilty when he doesn't have dynamic surges of desire. Powerful Choleric will accept what's profitable and throw away the rest with no guilt, but he should realize the temperament differences and not scoff at those who don't act out his role and follow his lead.

The second reason we don't achieve lasting results from even inspired instruction is that we don't have the power within us to conduct supernatural transformations. We need *spiritual* energy, and yet most of us don't know where to find it. We may mumble mantras, put statues on our dashboards, donate dollars to the disabled, sew for the heathen, and take trips to the Himalayas, but somehow we don't feel much different inside.

Find Spiritual Energy

My husband and I, after losing two brain-damaged sons, were searching. We were achieving on the surface but we were hurting underneath. We began looking for answers to life. Fred went to the library and took out books on religion, and we tried to find a desirable denomination. Little did we know at the time that religion and denominations don't change lives. Gratefully, each one of us, within a year, at different times and in different places, was presented with the claims of Christ as a catalyst to change. "But as many as received him, to them gave he power to become the sons of God, even to them that believe on his name" (John 1:12).

We needed *power*; we *believed* in the Lord Jesus; we *received* Him into our hearts. Romans 12:1 and 2 gave us direction:

. . . present your bodies a living sacrifice, holy, acceptable unto God, which is your reasonable service.

And be not conformed to this world: but be ye transformed by the renewing of your mind, that ye may prove [know] what is that good, and acceptable, and perfect, will of God.

Present Your Bodies

Total being, time, mind, soul, temperament, strengths, and weaknesses. Say, "Here it is Lord; it's all Yours. Do with me what You will."

Be Not Conformed to This World

Don't let my eyes focus only on earthly pleasures. Let me realize how transitory possessions and prestige really are.

Be Ye Transformed by the Renewing of Your Mind

Here is the hope. It is possible for the Spirit of the Lord in my life to make me over, to brighten and refresh my mind. *Then* (a connector word)—*then*, after I have presented my whole life to the Lord; moved my aim from the flesh to the Spirit; allowed the Lord to renew my tired mind—*then ye may know.* . . . What a strong word *know*. There's not much in life we can be sure of. *Guess* or *hope*, but *know*? Yes, "Then you will know what is that good, acceptable, perfect will of God."

"You mean I can know what God wants for my life?"

Yes, you can know God's perfect will. Fred and I began to study the Bible and the personalities at the same time, and we were amazed at how well they fit together. As we began to study our own personality patterns, instead of trying to shape each other up (as we had tried to do for fifteen years), we found Scripture to encourage us. Nowhere did the Bible say I was responsible for Fred's behavior, or he was the judge of my actions. Instead we found instructions to examine ourselves, not others.

Galatians 6:4 GNB	Each one should judge his own conduct . . .
1 Corinthians 11:28 GNB	Everyone should examine himself . . .
2 Corinthians 13:5 GNB	Put yourselves to the test and judge yourselves . . .

Psalm 26:1, 2 KJV   Judge me, O Lord. . . . Examine me, O Lord, and prove me; try my reins and my heart.

Paraphrase of Psalm 139:23, 24   Search me, oh God, and know my heart—what is way inside, the real me—try me, test me and know my ways—how I behave and get along with others. If there be any offensive way in me—actions and moods that offend or hurt other people—please help me to change.

We began to search our hearts and analyze ourselves, using the tool of the temperaments. As we brought couples into our home and shared what little we knew, we saw changes in ourselves and others.

Our Uniqueness

We learned God did not make us all alike. Each one of us is unique. Paul tells us that we should examine ourselves and find out what gifts God has given us and what weaknesses He wishes us to overcome with our willingness and His power. Paul compares us to a body where Christ is the head and we are the parts:

> Under his control all the different parts of the body fit together, and the whole body is held together by every joint with which it is provided. So when each separate part works as it should, the whole body grows and builds itself up through love. (Eph. 4:16 GNB)

God made each one of us different, so we could function in our own role. He made some of us to be *feet*—to move, to administer, to accomplish, like Powerful Choleric. He made some of us to be *minds*—to think deeply, to feel, to write, like Perfect Melancholy. He made some of us to be *hands*—to serve, to smooth, to soothe, like Peaceful Phlegmatic. He made some of us to be *mouths*—to talk, to teach, to encourage, like Popular Sanguine.

> Now hath God set the members, every one of them in the body, as it hath pleased him. (1 Cor. 12:18)

God could have made us all Popular Sanguines. We would have lots of fun but accomplish little.

He could have made us all Perfect Melancholies. We would have been organized and charted but not very cheerful.

He could have made us all Powerful Cholerics. We would have been all set to lead, but impatient that no one would follow.

He could have made us all Peaceful Phlegmatics. We would have had a peaceful world but not much enthusiasm for life.

We need each temperament for the total function of the body. Each part should do its work to unify the action and produce harmonious results.

Parts Are Not Enough

What if we have all these parts available—all doing their own thing—but Christ is not in control? What if Popular Sanguines are talking, Perfect Melancholies are thinking, Powerful Cholerics are doing, and Peaceful Phlegmatics are mediating, but they are operating without any spiritual depth? There will be no unity of purpose. There will be no coordination of results. For the parts to function as they should, we need Christ in our lives.

I learned this principle personally through the experience with my two brain-damaged sons. Each one was beautiful to look at. They had bright-blue eyes, blond hair, turned-up noses, dimpled chins. They had normal arms and legs that moved, but they did not have normal brains. They had all their parts, but there was no master control. They had eyes but they could not see; ears but they could not hear; hands but they could not hold; feet but they could not walk. They looked all right on the outside, but without a brain, nothing worked.

A lot of us are like my boys—we look all right on the outside, but without Christ as our head, nothing much is working. Paul says, "All I want is to know Christ and to experience the power of his resurrection, to share in his sufferings and become like him . . . " (Phil. 3:10 GNB).

Your Best Friend

Have you ever had a friend whom you loved so much that you wanted to be with him all the time and get to know him better every day? Has his presence lit up your life, so you felt energized, just being close? Have you cared so much for him that you were willing to bear his burdens and stand in for him in times of trouble? Have you watched him so closely and followed him so much that you've almost become like him? Jesus wants that kind of relationship with you. He wants you to get to know Him better by reading His words and talking to Him; He wants you to feel His power in your life, so you can overcome your weakness. He wants you to realize He suffered, just as you do, and He wants to spend so much time together that you become like Him.

If you wanted to become like Him, you would aim to amplify your strengths and eliminate your weaknesses, for Jesus had the best of each temperament. He had the storytelling gifts of Popular Sanguine, the depth and sensitivity of Perfect Melancholy, the administrative ability of Powerful Choleric, and the calm nature of Peaceful Phlegmatic.

Jesus lives today in the hearts of all believers, so as you put your personal plan for improvement into action, make sure you're connected to the source of *Power* to make it all possible. "The Lord hath done great things for us . . . " (Ps. 126:3).

Personality Plus Power Produces Positive People

Personality Test Word Definitions

Adapted from *Personality Patterns* by Lana Bateman, published by Huntington House, Inc., Lafayette, LA.

STRENGTHS

1

Adventurous. One who will take on new and daring enterprises with a determination to master them.
Adaptable. Easily fits and is comfortable in any situation.
Animated. Full of life, lively use of hand, arm, and face gestures.
Analytical. Likes to examine the parts for their logical and proper relationships.

2

Persistent. Sees one project through to its completion before starting another.
Playful. Full of fun and good humor.
Persuasive. Convinces through logic and fact rather than charm or power.
Peaceful. Seems undisturbed and tranquil and retreats from any form of strife.

3

Submissive. Easily accepts any other's point of view or desire with little need to assert his own opinion.
Self-sacrificing. Willingly gives up his own personal being for the sake of, or to meet the needs of others.
Sociable. One who sees being with others as an opportunity to be cute and entertaining rather than as a challenge or business opportunity.
Strong-willed. One who is determined to have his own way.

4

Considerate. Having regard for the needs and feelings of others.

Controlled. Has emotional feelings but rarely displays them.

Competitive. Turns every situation, happening, or game into a contest and always plays to win!

Convincing. Can win you over to anything through the sheer charm of his personality.

5

Refreshing. Renews and stimulates or makes others feel good.

Respectful. Treats others with deference, honor, and esteem.

Reserved. Self-restraint in expression of emotion or enthusiasm.

Resourceful. Able to act quickly and effectively in virtually all situations.

6

Satisfied. A person who easily accepts any circumstance or situation.

Sensitive. Intensively cares about others, and what happens.

Self-reliant. An independent person who can fully rely on his own capabilities, judgment, and resources.

Spirited. Full of life and excitement.

7

Planner. Prefers to work out a detailed arrangement beforehand for the accomplishment of project or goal, and prefers involvement with the planning stages and the finished product rather than the carrying out of the task.

Patient. Unmoved by delay, remains calm and tolerant.

Positive. Knows it will turn out right if he's in charge.

Promoter. Urges or compels others to go along, join, or invest through the charm of his own personality.

8

Sure. Confident, rarely hesitates or wavers.

Spontaneous. Prefers all of life to be impulsive, unpremeditated activity, not restricted by plans.

Scheduled. Makes, and lives, according to a daily plan, dislikes his plan to be interrupted.

Shy. Quiet, doesn't easily instigate a conversation.

9

Orderly. A person who has a methodical, systematic arrangement of things.

Obliging. Accommodating. One who is quick to do it another's way.

Outspoken. Speaks frankly and without reserve.

Optimistic. Sunny disposition who convinces himself and others that everything will turn out all right.

10

Friendly. A responder rather than an initiator, seldom starts a conversation.

Faithful. Consistently reliable, steadfast, loyal, and devoted sometimes beyond reason.

Funny. Sparkling sense of humor that can make virtually any story into an hilarious event.

Forceful. A commanding personality whom others would hesitate to take a stand against.

11

Daring. Willing to take risks; fearless, bold.

Delightful. A person who is upbeat and fun to be with.

Diplomatic. Deals with people tactfully, sensitively, and patiently.

Detailed. Does everything in proper order with a clear memory of all the things that happen.

12

Cheerful. Consistently in good spirits and promoting happiness in others.

Consistent. Stays emotionally on an even keel, responding as one might expect.

Cultured. One whose interests involve both intellectual and artistic pursuits, such as theater, symphony, ballet.

Confident. Self-assured and certain of own ability and success.

13

Idealistic. Visualizes things in their perfect form, and has a need to measure up to that standard himself.

Independent. Self-sufficient, self-supporting, self-confident, and seems to have little need of help.

Inoffensive. A person who never says or causes anything unpleasant or objectionable.

Inspiring. Encourages others to work, join, or be involved, and makes the whole thing fun.

14

Demonstrative. Openly expresses emotion, especially affection and doesn't hesitate to touch others while speaking to them.

Decisive. A person with quick, conclusive, judgment-making ability.

Dry humor. Exhibits "dry wit," usually one-liners which can be sarcastic in nature.

Deep. Intense and often introspective with a distaste for surface conversation and pursuits.

15

Mediator. Consistently finds him- or herself in the role of reconciling differences in order to avoid conflict.

Musical. Participates in or has a deep appreciation for music, is committed to music as an art form, rather than the fun of performance.

Mover. Driven by a need to be productive, is a leader whom others follow, finds it difficult to sit still.

Mixes easily. Loves a party and can't wait to meet everyone in the room, never meets a stranger.

16

Thoughtful. A considerate person who remembers special occasions and is quick to make a kind gesture.

Tenacious. Holds on firmly, stubbornly, and won't let go until the goal is accomplished.

Talker. Constantly talking, generally telling funny stories and entertaining everyone around, feeling the need to fill the silence in order to make others comfortable.

Tolerant. Easily accepts the thoughts and ways of others without the need to disagree with or change them.

17

Listener. Always seems willing to hear what you have to say.

Loyal. Faithful to a person, ideal, or job, sometimes beyond reason.

Leader. A natural born director, who is driven to be in charge, and often finds it difficult to believe that anyone else can do the job as well.

Lively. Full of life, vigorous, energetic.

18

Contented. Easily satisfied with what he has, rarely envious.

Chief. Commands leadership and expects people to follow.

Chartmaker. Organizes life, tasks, and problem solving by making lists, forms, or graphs.

Cute. Precious, adorable, center of attention.

19

Perfectionist. Places high standards on himself, and often on others, desiring that everything be in proper order at all times.

Pleasant. Easygoing, easy to be around, easy to talk with.

Productive. Must constantly be working or achieving, often finds it very difficult to rest.

Popular. Life of the party and therefore much desired as a party guest.

20

Bouncy. A bubbly, lively personality, full of energy.

Bold. Fearless, daring, forward, unafraid of risk.

Behaved. Consistently desires to conduct himself within the realm of what he feels is proper.

Balanced. Stable, middle-of-the-road personality, not subject to sharp highs or lows.

WEAKNESSES

21

Blank. A person who shows little facial expression or emotion.

Bashful. Shrinks from getting attention, resulting from self-consciousness.

Brassy. Showy, flashy, comes on strong, too loud.

Bossy. Commanding, domineering, sometimes overbearing in adult relationships.

22

Undisciplined. A person whose lack of order permeates most every area of his life.

Unsympathetic. Finds it difficult to relate to the problems or hurts of others.

Unenthusiastic. Tends to not get excited, often feeling it won't work anyway.

Unforgiving. One who has difficulty forgiving or forgetting a hurt or injustice done to them, apt to hold onto a grudge.

23

Reticent. Unwilling or struggles against getting involved, especially when complex.

Resentful. Often holds ill feelings as a result of real or imagined offenses.

Resistant. Strives, works against, or hesitates to accept any other way but his own.

Repetitious. Retells stories and incidents to entertain you without realizing he has already told the story several times before, is constantly needing something to say.

24

Fussy. Insistent over petty matters or details, calling for great attention to trivial details.

Fearful. Often experiences feelings of deep concern, apprehension, or anxiousness.

Forgetful. Lack of memory which is usually tied to a lack of discipline and not bothering to mentally record things that aren't fun.

Frank. Straightforward, outspoken, and doesn't mind telling you exactly what he thinks.

25

Impatient. A person who finds it difficult to endure irritation or wait for others.

Insecure. One who is apprehensive or lacks confidence.

Indecisive. The person who finds it difficult to make any decision at all. (Not the personality that labors long over each decision in order to make the perfect one.)

Interrupts. A person who is more of a talker than a listener, who starts speaking without even realizing someone else is already speaking.

26

Unpopular. A person whose intensity and demand for perfection can push others away.

Uninvolved. Has no desire to listen or become interested in clubs, groups, activities, or other people's lives.

Unpredictable. May be ecstatic one moment and down the next, or willing to help but then disappears, or promises to come but forgets to show up.

Unaffectionate. Finds it difficult to verbally or physically demonstrate tenderness openly.

27

Headstrong. Insists on having his own way.

Haphazard. Has no consistent way of doing things.

Hard to please. A person whose standards are set so high that it is difficult to ever satisfy them.

Hesitant. Slow to get moving and hard to get involved.

28

Plain. A middle-of-the-road personality without highs or lows and showing little, if any, emotion.

Pessimistic. While hoping for the best, this person generally sees the downside of a situation first.

Proud. One with great self-esteem who sees himself as always right and the best person for the job.

Permissive. Allows others (including children) to do as they please in order to keep from being disliked.

29

Angered easily. One who has a childlike flash-in-the-pan temper that expresses itself in tantrum style and is over and forgotten almost instantly.

Aimless. Not a goal-setter with little desire to be one.

Argumentative. Incites arguments generally because he is right, no matter what the situation may be.

Alienated. Easily feels estranged from others, often because of insecurity or fear that others don't really enjoy his company.

30

Naive. Simple and childlike perspective, lacking sophistication or comprehension of what the deeper levels of life are really about.

Negative attitude. One whose attitude is seldom positive and is often able to see only the down or dark side of each situation.

Nervy. Full of confidence, fortitude, and sheer guts, often in a negative sense.

Nonchalant. Easygoing, unconcerned, indifferent.

31

Worrier. Consistently feels uncertain, troubled, or anxious.

Withdrawn. A person who pulls back to himself and needs a great deal of alone or isolation time.

Workaholic. An aggressive goal-setter who must be constantly productive and feels very guilty when resting, is not driven by a need for perfection or completion but by a need for accomplishment and reward.

Wants credit. Thrives on the credit or approval of others. As an entertainer this person feeds on the applause, laughter, and/or acceptance of an audience.

32

Too sensitive. Overly introspective and easily offended when misunderstood.

Tactless. Sometimes expresses himself in a somewhat offensive and inconsiderate way.

Timid. Shrinks from difficult situations.

Talkative. An entertaining, compulsive talker who finds it difficult to listen.

33

Doubtful. Characterized by uncertainty and lack of confidence that it will ever work out.

Disorganized. Lack of ability to ever get life in order.

Domineering. Compulsively takes control of situations and/or people, usually telling others what to do.

Depressed. A person who feels down much of the time.

34

Inconsistent. Erratic, contradictory, with actions and emotions not based on logic.

Introvert. A person whose thoughts and interests are directed inward, lives within himself.

Intolerant. Appears unable to withstand or accept another's attitudes, point of view, or way of doing things.

Indifferent. A person to whom most things don't matter one way or the other.

35

Messy. Living in a state of disorder, unable to find things.

Moody. Doesn't get very high emotionally, but easily slips into low lows, often when feeling unappreciated.

Mumbles. Will talk quietly under the breath when pushed, doesn't bother to speak clearly.

Manipulative. Influences or manages shrewdly or deviously for his own advantage, *will* get his way somehow.

36

Slow. Doesn't often act or think quickly, too much of a bother.

Stubborn. Determined to exert his or her own will, not easily persuaded, obstinate.

Show-off. Needs to be the center of attention, wants to be watched.

Skeptical. Disbelieving, questioning the motive behind the words.

37

Loner. Requires a lot of private time and tends to avoid other people.

Lord over. Doesn't hesitate to let you know that he is right or is in control.

Lazy. Evaluates work or activity in terms of how much energy it will take.

Loud. A person whose laugh or voice can be heard above others in the room.

38

Sluggish. Slow to get started, needs push to be motivated.

Suspicious. Tends to suspect or distrust others or ideas.

Short-tempered. Has a demanding impatience-based anger and a short fuse. Anger is expressed when others are not moving fast enough or have not completed what they have been asked to do.

Scatterbrained. Lacks the power of concentration or attention, flighty.

39

Revengeful. Knowingly or otherwise holds a grudge and punishes the offender, often by subtly withholding friendship or affection.

Restless. Likes constant new activity because it isn't fun to do the same things all the time.

Reluctant. Unwilling or struggles against getting involved.

Rash. May act hastily, without thinking things through, generally because of impatience.

40

Compromising. Will often relax his position, even when right, in order to avoid conflict.

Critical. Constantly evaluating and making judgments, frequently thinking or expressing negative reactions.

Crafty. Shrewd, one who can always find a way to get to the desired end.

Changeable. A childlike, short attention span that needs a lot of change and variety to keep from getting bored.